JACOB LAGUERRE

NLP Handbook

The 80/20 of Neuro-linguistic Programming

First published by Power Creativity Influence, LLC 2024

Copyright © 2024 by Jacob Laguerre

All rights reserved. No part of this publication may be reproduced, stored or transmitted in any form or by any means, electronic, mechanical, photocopying, recording, scanning, or otherwise without written permission from the publisher. It is illegal to copy this book, post it to a website, or distribute it by any other means without permission.

Designations used by companies to distinguish their products are often claimed as trademarks. All brand names and product names used in this book and on its cover are trade names, service marks, trademarks and registered trademarks of their respective owners. The publishers and the book are not associated with any product or vendor mentioned in this book. None of the companies referenced within the book have endorsed the book.

The information provided in this book is intended for educational purposes only. It is not a substitute for professional advice or expert guidance. The author and publisher does not assume any responsibility or liability for the accuracy, completeness, or usefulness of the information provided. Readers are encouraged to seek professional advice or consult subject matter experts for their specific concerns.

First edition

ISBN: 9781666406849

This book was professionally typeset on Reedsy.
Find out more at reedsy.com

Contents

Acknowledgement	vi
HOLD YOUR HORSES!	vii
What People Say About PCI Alpha	viii
Chapter 1: The Foundations of NLP	1
History of NLP	1
NLP Model	2
NLP Presuppositions	4
The 4 Operational Principles	11
Well-Formedness Conditions	12
Chapter 2: The Original Models of NLP	15
Milton Erickson	15
Virginia Satir	19
Fritz Perls	27
Chapter 3: Attitude is Everything	31
The NLP Attitude	31
Elements of Attitude	37
Chapter 4: How We Think & Experience	45
NLP Communication Model	45
Neurological Levels	48
NLP Representational Systems	51
Eye-Accessing Cues	56
Strategies 101	59
Time-lines	61
Hierarchy of Ideas	65
NLP Frames	67

Meta-Programs	73
Chapter 5: NLP Modeling	78
Introduction	78
Basic Principles of Modeling	79
Modeling Methodology	85
Modeling Strategies	100
Code Congruence	108
Chapter 6: The Key Language Models	111
Meta Model	111
The Meta Model Revisited	134
Milton Model	168
Sleight of Mouth	182
Chapter 7: NLP Anchoring	190
Anchoring Fundamentals	190
State Elicitation	192
Stacking Anchors vs. Chaining Anchors	194
How to Use Anchoring in Persuasion	198
NLP Anchoring Best Practices	201
Chapter 8: Meta-States	203
What are Meta-States?	203
Crash Course on States	206
Beyond Primary States	213
Texturing States	215
The Anatomy of Meta-States	218
The Meta-Stating Process	226
Chapter 9: The Matrix Model	236
Matrix 101	236
Matrix 102	248
Grounding Matrix	255
States Matrix	255
Meta-States & The Matrix	262

Process Matrices	265
Meaning Matrix	265
Intention Matrix	274
Content Matrices	280
Self Matrix	280
Power Matrix	287
Others Matrix	292
Time Matrix	294
World Matrix	298
Chapter 10: NLP Certifications	301
SNLP	301
IBCP	304
ABH-NLP	313
INLPTA	319
AIP	330
Bibliography	336
About the Author	337

Acknowledgement

I would like to thank all of the NLPers who came before me and shared their knowledge over the years to help make this book possible. I would first like to thank Richard Bandler and John Grinder, the co-founders of NLP, for creating this field in the first place. I would also like to thank other prominent NLPers including Robert Dilts, L. Michael Hall, Michael Breen, Eric Robbie, Leslie Cameron-Bandler, and Wyatt Woodsmall, for their invaluable contributions to the field of NLP. I stood on the shoulders of these giants as I put this book together.

HOLD YOUR HORSES!

Before you start diving into the contents of this book, I highly recommend downloading our free NLP mind map over at:

pcialpha.com/mindmap

It takes just a few seconds and it'll be sent to your inbox in a jiffy. This will be a useful resource to have on hand as you're reading the book.

What People Say About PCI Alpha

"I have been keenly reading all the news and sharing knowledge by PCI for a long time. Training myself to put to use the NLP, I find that PCI shares great insights to NLP, objectively stated, clear in their perspective and totally unbiased sharing. No wonder, I don't miss any of their knowledge sharing. Thank you for keeping my mind ignited for more."

— Geeta Varma, Independent HR Consultant

"I've benefited from your emails and blogs. There's a lot of value about NLP and coaching that I can apply not only with my clients but also with myself. I really appreciate your valuable work that help transform people lives."

— Pawinee, Coach

"Receiving the PCI Alpha newsletter is like having a dedicated NLP curator. The content is well-structured, easy to understand, and provides a bridge between the theory of NLP and its real-world applications.It has been an invaluable asset in keeping me informed and inspired.I recommend PCI Alpha's newsletter to

anyone passionate about NLP."

— Gary Tintinger, Newsletter Subscriber

"*Jacob Laguerre's email course has been incredibly insightful. Each email is a lesson in itself, thoughtfully crafted and packed with valuable NLP strategies. I especially love how Jacob uses storytelling to drive home the message. I've enjoyed and benefited from every single email since 2022. Thank you, Jacob!*"

— Fiona Lok, Sales Trainer

"*Love your work, and all you are doing for NLP, I super enjoy your daily feeds with insights into NLP. I have purchased your courses before and they are awesome, I really enjoyed the Meta Programs, a deep and delicious study!*"

— Kathy Welter, Co-Owner of Welter Nichols and Associates

Chapter 1: The Foundations of NLP

History of NLP

Neuro-linguistic Programming, or NLP for short, started in the 1970s over at the University of California. At the time, John Grinder was an assistant professor at the university and Richard Bandler was a psychology student. He was also interested in psychotherapy.

Bandler started off by modeling Virginia Satir and Fritz Perls. Both of them were highly successful therapists in their own right. Virginia Satir was a world-renowned family therapist who was able to resolve difficult family relationships that others found nearly impossible. Fritz Perls was an established psychotherapist and the originator of a school of therapy known as Gestalt. Bandler used Fritz Perls' Gestalt therapy and formed study groups and began holding workshops centered around Gestalt therapy.

Later on, John and Richard also modeled Milton Erickson. Milton Erickson was a world-famous hypnotherapist and is considered by many to be the founding father of Modern Hypnotherapy. He was known for his use of indirect suggestion, metaphor, and storytelling to induce trance and facilitate change in his clients.

Between 1975 and 1977, they published their initial findings in the Structure of Magic Vol. 1 and 2, which was based on the techniques of Fritz Perls and Virginia Satir, and the Patterns of the Hypnotic Techniques of Milton Erickson Vol. 1 and Vol. 2. They were originally intended to be used by therapists when working with their clients and were later recognized as seminal works in Neuro-linguistic Programming.

* * *

NLP Model

To understand NLP, let's first break down each letter.

N stands for Neuro, which refers to how we process our experiences through the 5 senses. These senses each map to a representational system. Representational systems are our internal systems for how we re-present experience in our "internal screen". In NLP, there are 5 main representational systems that we look at: Visual, Auditory, Kinesthetic, Olfactory, and Gustatory.

Visual is what we see. For example, when you think of a car, you may see an image of a car in your mind, or recall a specific color, shape, or model of a car.

Auditory is what we hear. For example, when you think of a car, you may hear the sound of the engine, the horn, or the music playing inside.

Kinesthetic is what we can feel. For example, when you think of a car, you may feel the sensation of driving, the temperature, the texture, or the emotion associated with the car.

Olfactory is what we can smell. For example, when you think of a car, you may smell the gasoline, the leather, or the air freshener.

Gustatory is what we can taste. For example, when you think of a car, you may taste the coffee, the gum, or the food that you ate in the car.

Most people have a preferred representational system that's either Visual, Auditory, or Kinesthetic. This means that they tend to process information more easily and effectively through one of these senses. Knowing your own and others' preferred representational systems can help you communicate better and build rapport.

L stands for Linguistic, which refers to language and non-verbal processes that we use to give meaning to our representations. Language is not only a way of expressing our thoughts, but also a way of shaping them. The words we choose, the tone we use, the gestures we make, and the questions we ask can all influence how we perceive and respond to reality. NLP teaches us how to use language more effectively and precisely to achieve our desired outcomes.

P stands for Programming, which is the act of creating systematic responses. Programming is the way we organize our thoughts, feelings, and actions to produce certain results. We all have programs that run automatically in our mind, such as habits, routines, skills, strategies, etc. Some of these programs are beneficial, while others are outdated and ineffective. NLP helps us change our programs to suit our current needs and goals.

The NLP Patterns is what we use to program ourselves to get better results in life. These are the techniques that help us change our behavior, beliefs, emotions, and identity.

As you can see, NLP is a model made up of 3 components. By learning how these components work together, you put yourself in a position to attain excellence. NLP is not only a theory but also a practice. The best way to learn NLP is to apply it to your own life and experience the results for yourself.

* * *

NLP Presuppositions

NLP Presuppositions are useful filters for viewing the world. They're neither true nor false. But, if you were to adopt these presuppositions "as if" they were true, it can produce dramatic changes in how you view the world and how you relate to other people.

The meaning of communication is the response one gets.

In communication, it's usually assumed that one is transferring information to another person. One has information which "means" something to them and intends that the other person understand what they intend to communicate. Frequently one assumes that if they "say what they mean to say," then their responsibility for the communication is over.

If you want to be an effective communicator, you must realize that your responsibility does not end when you finish talking. For practical purposes, what you communicate is what the other person thinks you say and not what you intend to say. Often the two are quite different.

In communication, it is what the other person thinks that one says and how they respond to it that is important. This requires that you pay attention to the response that you're getting. If this is not the response that you want, then you need to change your communication until you get the desired response.

The map is not the territory.

Good communicators realize that the representations which they use to organize their experience of the world is not the same as the world.

It is important to distinguish between several semantic levels. The first semantic level is the external world. The second semantic level is one's experience of the world. This experience is one's "map" or "model" of the world and is different for each person. Each person creates a unique model of the world and thus lives in a somewhat different reality than everyone else.

One does not operate directly on the world but on one's experience of it. This experience may or may not be correct. To the extent that one's experience has a similar structure with the world it is correct and this accounts for its usefulness.

One's model of the world determines how one will perceive the world and what choices one will see as available to them. Many NLP techniques involve changing one's model of the world to make it more useful and to bring it more in line with the way the world is.

Language is a secondary representation of experience.

Language is the third semantic level after the external world and one's representation of the world, respectively.

Language is not experience but a representation of experience. Words are merely arbitrary tokens used to represent things one sees, hears, or feels. People who speak other languages use different words to represent the same things that English speakers see, hear or feel.

Also, since each person has a unique set of things that they have seen, heard, and felt in their lives, their words have different meanings to each of them. To the degree that these meanings are similar people can communicate effectively. When there are more differences than similarities, then problems begin to arise.

We can use language patterns like the "Sleight of Mouth" model (more on that later) to help us speak more concisely as well as create positive change in others.

Mind and body are parts of the same cybernetic system which affect one another.

Mind and body both refer to aspects of the same "whole" or "gestalt". They act as one and they influence each other in such a way that there is no separation. Anything that happens in one part of a cybernetic

CHAPTER 1: THE FOUNDATIONS OF NLP

system like a human being will affect all other parts of the system. This means that what you think affects how you feel and that the condition of your physical body affects how you think.

Your perceptual input, internal thought process, emotional process, physiological response and behavioral output all occur both simultaneously and through time. In practical terms, this means that you can change how you think by either directly changing how you think or by changing your physiology or feelings.

Law of Requisite Variety: In any cybernetic system, the element or person with the widest range of behaviors, variability, or choice will control the system.

Control in human systems refers to the ability to influence the quality of one's own and other people's experience in the moment and through time. The person with the greatest flexibility of behavior, i.e. number of ways of interacting, will control that system. Choice is always preferable to no choice and more choice is generally more preferable than less choice.

Behavior is geared towards adaptation.

One's behavior is determined by the context in which that behavior originates. One's reality is defined by one's perceptions of the world. The behavior that one exhibits is appropriate to their reality. All of one's behavior whether good or bad is an adaptation.

Everything is useful in some context. All behavior is, or was, adaptive given the context in which it was learned. In another context it may not be appropriate. People need to realize this and change their behavior when it is appropriate to do so.

Present behavior represents the best choice available to that person.

Under every behavior lies a positive intent. When you take into account who a person is, based on all of their life experiences and the choices that they are aware of, they make the best choice available to them at any moment in time. If they are given a better choice, they will take it.

In order to change someone's inappropriate behavior, it is necessary to give them other choices. Once this is done they will behave accordingly. Neuro-linguistic Programming has techniques for providing additional choices. Also, in Neuro-linguistic Programming, one never takes away choices from their clients, nor anyone else for that matter. One only provides more choices and explicitly contextualizes the existing choices.

Behavior is to be evaluated and appreciated or changed as appropriate in the context presented.

We need to evaluate other people's behavior in terms of what they are capable of becoming. One needs to strive to be all they are capable of being.

People have all of the resources they need to make the changes they want.

The task is to locate or access those resources and to make them available in the appropriate context. Neuro-linguistic Programming provides techniques to accomplish this task. What this means is that in practice people do not need to waste time trying to gain insight into

CHAPTER 1: THE FOUNDATIONS OF NLP

their problems or in developing resources to deal with their problems. They already have all the resources which they need to deal with their problems. All that is necessary is to access these resources and transfer them to the current time frame.

Possible in the world and possible for me is only a matter of how.

If any other human being is capable of performing some behavior then it is possible for you to also perform it. The process of determining "how" they do it is called "modeling" and is the process by which Neuro-linguistic Programming came into being in the first place.

The highest-quality information about other people is behavioral.

Listen to what people say but pay more attention to what they do. If there is any contradiction between the two, then rely on the behavior.

It is useful to make a distinction between behavior and self.

Just because one "screws up" on something, does not mean that they are a "screw up." Behavior is what a person says, does or feels at any moment in time. This does not equate to one's self. A person's self is greater than their behaviors.

There is no such thing as failure, there is only feedback.

It is much more valuable to view one's experience in terms of a learning frame than in terms of a failure frame. If a person does not succeed in something, this does not mean that they have failed. It just means that they have discovered one way not to do that particular thing. One then needs to vary their behavior until they find a way to succeed.

The person who sets the frame for the communication controls the communicating.

All of us have mental frames that we carry around in our heads. Our mental frames determine not only what we look at but how we look at things. Frames play an important role in communication and the person who sets the frame will usually control the interaction. Examples of frames include "win-win" frame, "win-lose" frame, religious frame, gossip frame, and so on.

Resistance indicates a lack of rapport.

When a client is not responding the way you would like, it is your responsibility to take ownership of their response and to alter your behavior accordingly. Be flexible in your approach and find a way to get on the same page as your client. You do not need to flee at the first sign of trouble. For some people, establishing rapport is more challenging than for others, but it is possible. Keep saying words that match their internal state and don't give up without a fight.

Humans can experience one-trial learning.

The human body is a true natural marvel. It can learn things with radical efficiency under the right circumstances. For example, if you throw a boy into the water and he doesn't know how to swim, he may grow up being afraid of the water for the rest of his life. NLP allows us to tap into our ability to learn things quickly to create near-instant change in almost any aspect of our lives.

* * *

CHAPTER 1: THE FOUNDATIONS OF NLP

The 4 Operational Principles

Neuro-linguistic programming is based on 4 operational principles that guide the practice and application of NLP techniques. These principles are essential for anyone who wants to master NLP and use it effectively in their own life and with others.

The first operational principle is to know your outcome. You need to have a clear and specific goal in mind for what you want to achieve, whether it is a personal change, a professional success, or a desired outcome with another person. Knowing your outcome gives you a direction and a purpose for your actions. Without knowing your outcome, you're like a ship without a compass, drifting aimlessly in the sea of possibilities.

The second operational principle is to have sufficient sensory acuity to know whether or not you're getting closer. This is the ability to notice the subtle changes and feedback that occur as you move towards your outcome. Sensory acuity is the skill of paying attention to the signals that your senses provide you, such as visual, auditory, kinesthetic, olfactory, and gustatory cues.

The third operational principle is to have sufficient flexibility of behavior so that you can vary your behavior until you get your desired outcome. This means you can adapt your behavior and approach according to the situation and the feedback you receive. Flexibility of behavior is the key to overcoming obstacles and challenges that arise as you pursue your outcome. Flexibility of behavior is also based on the presupposition of the "Law of Requisite Variety", which states that the system or person with the most flexibility will control the system or person with the least flexibility.

The fourth operational principle is to take action now. If you want things to happen, then you must have the willingness and courage to take action in the present. Action is the bridge between your intention and reality. Without action, your outcome will remain a dream or wish. Taking action now means you don't procrastinate, hesitate, or wait for perfect conditions to start. You take the first step and then the next one, and you keep moving forward until you reach your destination.

* * *

Well-Formedness Conditions

Well-Formedness Conditions are a set of criteria that help us formulate outcomes that are more realistic, specific, and congruent with our values and goals. These conditions are based on the idea that the language we use shapes our reality and influences our behavior. By following these conditions, we can ensure that our outcomes are clear, positive, and achievable. There are seven conditions in total.

The first condition is to state the outcome in positive terms. This means that we focus on what we want, rather than what we don't want. For example, instead of saying "I don't want to be stressed", we can say "I want to be calm and relaxed". The reason for this is that our mind cannot process negations directly. It has to first imagine what we don't want, and then try to avoid it. This creates a conflict between our conscious and subconscious mind, and makes it harder to achieve our desired state.

The second condition is to make sure that the outcome is within our control. This means that we can initiate and maintain the outcome by ourselves, without depending on other people or external factors. For example, instead of saying "I want my boss to appreciate me", we can say "I want to perform well at work and communicate my value to my boss". The reason for this is that we cannot control other people's thoughts, feelings, or actions. We can only control our own. By taking responsibility for our own outcome, we empower ourselves and increase our chances of success.

The third condition is to have a specific, sensory-based description of the outcome and the steps needed to get there. This means that we can see, hear, feel, taste, and smell what the outcome will be like, and how we will know when we have achieved it. For example, instead of saying "I want to be happy", we can say "I want to smile more, laugh more, and enjoy my hobbies". The reason for this is that vague and abstract outcomes are hard to measure and monitor. We need to have a clear picture of what we want, and a concrete plan of how to get there.

The fourth condition is to check for ecology. This means that we consider the impact of our outcome on ourselves and others, and make sure that it is aligned with our values and beliefs. For example, instead of saying "I want to be rich", we can say "I want to have enough money to live comfortably and support my family". The reason for this is that some outcomes may have negative consequences that outweigh the benefits. We need to make sure that our outcome is not only good for us, but also good for the people and the environment around us.

The fifth condition is to have more than one way to get the outcome.

This means that we are flexible and adaptable, and ready to change our strategy if needed. For example, instead of saying "I want to get a promotion by working hard", we can say "I want to get a promotion by working hard, or by taking a course, or by networking with the right people". The reason for this is that life is unpredictable and full of surprises. We may encounter obstacles, challenges, or opportunities that require us to adjust our course of action. By having multiple options, we increase our chances of reaching our destination.

The sixth condition is to specify the first step and make sure that it is achievable. This means that we break down our outcome into smaller, manageable steps, and start with the easiest one. For example, instead of saying "I want to write a book", we can say "I want to write a book, and the first step is to write an outline". The reason for this is that big and complex outcomes can be overwhelming and intimidating. We may feel discouraged or procrastinate if we don't know where to start. By taking one small step at a time, we build momentum and confidence, and move closer to our goal.

The seventh and final condition is to ask ourselves: does it increase choice? This means that we evaluate our outcome in terms of how it expands our possibilities and potential. For example, instead of saying "I want to lose weight", we can say "I want to lose weight, and this will give me more energy, more confidence, and more freedom". The reason for this is that the ultimate purpose of NLP is to help people have more choices in life. We don't want to limit ourselves or others by imposing rigid rules or expectations. We want to help ourselves and others discover new ways of being, doing, and having.

Chapter 2: The Original Models of NLP

Milton Erickson

> Every person's map of the world is as unique as their thumbprint. There are no two people alike. No two people who understand the same sentence the same way... So in dealing with people, you try not to fit them to your concept of what they should be.
> - Milton Erickson

Milton Erickson's career spanned more than 50 years and left a profound impact on the world of hypnosis, to the extent that many hypnotherapists use some form of his approach. He also had a major influence on the co-founders of Neuro-linguistic Programming.

Early Life

Milton Erickson was born on December 5, 1901 to Albert and Clara Erickson. He lived in a poor farming community with his 8 siblings. He was one of only 2 boys and had 7 sisters.

From a young age, his life seemed to be filled with trouble. He was late in learning how to speak and had trouble reading, which he believed was caused by dyslexia. Later on, he overcame his dyslexia during an auto-hypnotic experience. He said it was like a "blinding flash of light." He was also color blind and tone deaf. According to Erickson, he believed his "disabilities" helped him focus on the aspects of communication that other people tended to overlook.

When he turned 17, he contracted polio and was bed-ridden for an extended period of time. In a way, it was like a blessing in disguise. Being forced to lay in bed all day allowed him to be very observant, especially of his family members. He would take notice of their tone of voice, body language, facial expressions, and more.

He eventually trained his body to walk again. He embarked on a thousand-mile canoe trip by himself, which was both long and grueling. In the end, he still needed a cane to walk.

Milton's interest in hypnosis came at an early age. A traveling entertainer had passed through the area and performed some hypnotic techniques. At the time, Milton believed that hypnosis was too powerful a tool to be left to entertainers. He wanted to bring hypnosis into the realm of scientific evaluation and into the practice of medicine.

Later Life

It was Milton's family doctor that inspired him to become a physician. He attended the University of Wisconsin and received graduate degrees in psychology and medicine. He began his formal studies of hypnosis under Clark Hull. After a while, he realized that his ideas were somewhat different from Clark's.

CHAPTER 2: THE ORIGINAL MODELS OF NLP

He went on to take a series of positions at various state hospitals to continue his research. This also allowed him to refine his approach to therapy.

Many people are familiar with the idea of a "deep" trance, and early in his career Erickson was a pioneer in researching the unique and remarkable phenomena that are associated with that state, spending many hours at a time with individual subjects, deepening the trance.

He performed mental and physical examinations of soldiers during World War II. To help the war effort, the U.S. intelligence services enlisted him to meet with other experts about the psychological and mental factors that contribute to combat communication. During this time, he met with Gregory Bateson and Margaret Mead, and went on to form lifelong friendships with both of them. Through Gregory Bateson, he met Jay Haley and the future co-founders of NLP, Richard Bandler and John Grinder.

By the late 1930s, Erickson became renowned for his work in hypnosis. In 1957, he co-founded the American Society of Clinical Hypnosis with a number of his colleagues. He also served as the Inaugural President. In addition, he established the American Journal of Hypnosis, which is the official journal of the American Society of Clinical Hypnosis, and served as editor for 10 years.

In 1973, Jay Haley published Uncommon Therapy, and for the first time, Milton Erickson's approach was shared with people outside of the clinical hypnosis community. Erickson practically became an overnight celebrity, and people from all over the world wanted to meet him.

Not too long afterwards, he began holding teaching seminars which lasted until his death.

Milton Erickson's Approach

Milton had a very unique approach to hypnosis and medicine. Even though he was known as the world's leading hypnotist, he only used formal hypnosis in one-fifth of his cases in clinical practice.

He adapted his approach to each client. And his style was the complete opposite of traditional hypnosis. Unlike traditional hypnosis, which was direct and authoritarian, Milton's approach was indirect and permissive. For example, a classical hypnotist might say "You are going into a trance" while an Ericksonian hypnotist would say something like "you can comfortably learn how to go into a trance". With the Ericksonian approach, you're providing an opportunity for the subject to accept the suggestions they're most comfortable with, at their own pace, and with an awareness of the benefits.

Erickson firmly believed that it was not consciously possible to instruct the unconscious mind. Authoritarian suggestions are likely to be met with resistance. The unconscious mind is responsive to metaphors, opportunities, symbols, and contradictions.

According to Milton, everyone has a healthy, powerful core. It is the job of the hypnotist to help their client re-establish connection with their inner resources and to restore balance between the conscious and unconscious mind.

Fun Facts

- He was very interested in the walking styles of people.
- His motto was "observe, observe, observe". He even kept a notebook to make note of all of his observations.
- He was the first to describe the hand levitation method of induction.
- He could "utilize" anything about a client to help them change, including their beliefs, favorite words, cultural backgrounds, personal history, or even their neurotic habits.

* * *

Virginia Satir

Life is not the way it's supposed to be, it's the way it is. The way you cope with it is what makes the difference.
— Virginia Satir

Virginia Satir is globally recognized as the "Mother of Family Therapy". She was also a prolific author and one of the 3 original models of NLP, along with Milton Erickson and Fritz Perls.

She is also known for creating the Virginia Satir Change Model, which is a psychological model she developed through her clinical studies. This model became especially popular with the change management and organization gurus of the 1990s and 2000s to define how change impacts organizations.

Early Life

Virginia Satir was born on June 26, 1916 in Neillsville, Wisconsin. She was the oldest of five children born to Oscar Alfred Reinnard Pagenkopf and Minnie Happe Pagenkopf. From a young age, she was exceptionally bright. She taught herself how to read at age 3. By age 9, she had read all of the books in the library of her one-room school.

When she was 5 years old, she suffered from appendicitis. Her mother, being a devout Christian Scientist, refused to take her to a doctor. When her father was finally able to overrule her mother, her appendix had already ruptured. As a result, she had to stay in the hospital for several months.

She lived through the Great Depression while she was in her teens. During that time, she worked a part-time job to help ease the financial burden of her family. She also attended as many courses as possible so she could graduate early.

In 1932, she graduated from high school and immediately enrolled into Milwaukee State Teachers College, now called the University of Wisconsin. She paid for her education by working part-time at the Works Projects Administration, Gimbels Department store, and a bit of babysitting. She graduated with her bachelor's in 1936 and went on to become a teacher for a few years.

Later Life

During her time as a schoolteacher, she noticed that the involved and supportive parents not only helped students in the classroom but could also heal family dynamics. She started meeting and cooperating with

CHAPTER 2: THE ORIGINAL MODELS OF NLP

the parents of her students and began to see the family system as a reflection of the world at large. She even stated "If we can heal the family, we can heal the world."

In 1948, she received her master's degree from the University of Chicago School of Social Services Administration. Soon after, she started her own private practice. She met with her first family in her private practice in 1951.

A few years after she started her private practice, she was offered a position at the Illinois Psychiatric Institute. While she was there, she taught other therapists the importance of addressing the whole family during treatment, not just the individual. She realized that individual problems extend to the family and often stem from the family.

In 1959, she moved to California and helped to establish the Mental Research Institute. 3 years later, the MRI received a grant from NIMH, which is short for the National Institute of Mental Health. The grant allowed them to create the very first family therapy training program. Shortly after receiving the grant, Virginia was hired as the Training Director.

In 1964, Virginia published her first book titled "Conjoint Family Therapy." The book was based on the training manual she wrote while she was at the Mental Research Institute. After she published the book, her fame and recognition grew.

In the mid-1970s, she was discovered by the co-founders of NLP, Richard Bandler and John Grinder. It was through her work, along with Fritz Perls, that they were able to create the Meta Model. They even co-authored a book with Virginia called "Changing with Families", which bore the subtitle: "A Book About Further Education for Being Human."

Around the 1990s, Steve Andreas, one of Bandler and Grinder's students, wrote "Virginia Satir: The Patterns of Her Magic" where he summarized the major patterns of Satir's works.

Virginia had a strong passion for networking and connecting people. She wanted to help individuals connect with mental health workers or other people who suffered from diseases similar to their own. This led her to founding "Beautiful People" in 1970, which later became the International Human Learning Resources Network. In 1977, she founded the Avanta Network, which was renamed to the Virginia Satir Global Network in 2010. The organization exists today to carry on her work and promote her approach to therapy.

She died in 1988 of pancreatic cancer.

Satir Therapeutic Beliefs

Virginia Satir had a set of beliefs that enabled her to get amazing results for her clients. Here they are listed below:

- CHANGE is possible. Even if external change is limited, internal change is possible
- PARENTS do the best they can at any given time.
- WE all have the internal resources we need to cope successfully and to grow.
- WE have choices, especially in terms of responding to stress instead of reacting to

- situations.
- THERAPY needs to focus on health and possibilities instead of pathology.
- HOPE is a significant component or ingredient for change.
- PEOPLE connect on the basis of being similar and grow on the basis of being different.
- A major goal of therapy is to become our own choice makers.
- WE are all manifestations of the same life force.
- MOST people choose familiarity over comfort, especially during times of stress.
- THE problem is not the problem; coping is the problem.
- FEELINGS belong to us. We all have them.
- PEOPLE are basically good. To connect with and validate their own self-worth, they need to find their own inner treasure.
- PARENTS often repeat the familiar patterns from their growing up times, even if the
- patterns are dysfunctional.
- WE cannot change past events, only the effects they have on us.
- APPRECIATING and accepting the past increases our ability to manage our present.
- ONE goal in moving toward wholeness is to accept our parental figures as people and meet them at their level of personhood rather than only in their roles.
- COPING is the manifestation of our level of self-worth. The higher our self-worth, the more wholesome our coping.
- HUMAN processes are universal and therefore occur in different settings, cultures, and circumstances.
- PROCESS is the avenue of change. Content forms the context in which change can take place.
- CONGRUENCE and high self-esteem are major goals in the Satir model.

- HEALTHY human relationships are built on equality of value.

-Virginia Satir

Satir Categories

During her clinical studies, she came up with 5 different styles of communication known as the Satir Categories. 4 out of 5 were responsible for creating many conflicts while only one of them can be used for resolving conflict and bringing families together.

Blamer

Blamers are people who always find fault with someone or something. They almost never take responsibility for their actions. They put on a tough mask to hide their feelings of alienation and loneliness. They are the most likely to initiate conflict.

Placater (Non-assertive)

Placaters are what you would call a "people pleaser". They almost never disagree, are very non-assertive, and always seek approval. They're very concerned about how people view them.

Computer

People who exhibit Computer behavior often appear cold and unfeeling. Even if they don't display any emotion on the outside, there may be a firework of emotions on the inside. They often make value judgments without saying who made the judgment, which implies that everyone should agree.

Distractor

Distractors are attention-seekers. They do this to compensate for their feelings of loneliness and inadequacy. They will often change the subject and not answer a question directly. They will also cycle through the other categories as well.

Leveler

Levelers say what they mean and mean what they say. Their thoughts, words and actions are all in alignment. They relate well with others and know how to be assertive. It is the only communication category that can be used to resolve conflict and bring people together.

Satir Change Model

The Satir Change Model was created to help people analyze their situation and choices. A strong emphasis is placed on engaging the inner self. The model illustrates how people go through change and how they can cope with such change to improve their relationship with each other.

There are 5 stages in total:

First Stage: Late Status Quo

In this stage, the individual is in a familiar and predictable environment. Everyone is playing their part and knows what to expect, how to react, and how to behave. Things aren't necessarily great, but it isn't bad either.

Second Stage: Resistance

When we encounter something that challenges the status quo, we enter the Resistance Phase. This new element is called a foreign element. It's called foreign to represent the fact that it's outside the way of how things are normally done. A foreign element always requires a response.

Third Stage: Chaos

Once the foreign element reaches critical mass, we enter into the Chaos stage. The old way of doing things is no longer viable. It's normal to feel stressed, confused, or anxious during this time. Chaos is important because it helps to inspire creativity in individuals to find solutions.

Fourth Stage: Practice and Integration

New ideas are being implemented at this stage as the individuals determine what's the best way forward. Members may feel exhilarated as things start to click. More support may be needed at this stage compared to the previous one, especially if things don't work out the first time.

Final Stage: New Status Quo

The changes that were adopted in the previous stage have begun to take hold. What was once a new skill now becomes second nature. Everyone is much more centered and alert. It's important to celebrate success during this phase while remaining open to new ideas.

It should be noted that this process is not always linear. If individuals find a temporary coping skill or solution that does not bring the desired result, they may regress back to chaos.

* * *

Fritz Perls

> I do my thing and you do your thing.
> I am not in this world to live up to your expectations, and you are not in this world to live up to mine.
> You are you, and I am I, and if by chance we find each other, it's beautiful.
> If not, it can't be helped.
> — Fritz Perls

Friedrich Salomon Perls, better known as Fritz Perls, was a German-born psychiatrist, psychoanalyst, and therapist. He coined the term "Gestalt therapy", which is a form of psychotherapy he developed with his wife in the 1940s and 1950s. His approach is related to the Gestalt psychology and the Gestalt Theoretical Psychotherapy of Hans-Jurgen Walter. The interconnection between the individual being and the environment that he interacts with on a daily basis is the main idea behind Gestalt therapy.

Fritz Perls was born on July 8, 1893 in Berlin, Germany. His family expected him to practice law, like his uncle Herman Staub, but he studied medicine instead.

He joined the German army during World War I, and spent time in the trenches. After the war ended in 1918, he returned to his medical studies and graduated 2 years later, specializing in neuropsychiatry as a medical doctor. He then became an assistant to Kurt Goldstein, who was working with brain injured soldiers at the time. While he was there, Perls slowly developed an interest in psychoanalysis.

In 1927, Fritz Perls became a member of Wilhelm Reich's technical seminars in Vienna. Reich's concept of character analysis had a profound influence on Perls.

In 1930, Reich became Perls' supervising senior analyst in Berlin. That same year, he married Laura Perls (born Lore Posner), and they had 2 children: Renate and Stephen.

In 1933, Fritz Perls, his wife, and their eldest son Renate, were forced to leave Germany. At the time, Hitler had come into power and Perls was of Jewish descent and had participated in anti-fascist political activities in the past. They first went to the Netherlands, and one year later, they emigrated to South Africa. While he was there, Fritz Perls started a psychoanalytic training institute.

While in South Africa, Perls was influenced by Jan Smuts' "holism". It was also during this period that he co-wrote his first book "Ego, Hunger, and Aggression", which he published in 1942. His wife wrote two chapters of the book, however, when it was re-published in the United States she was not given any recognition for her work.

In 1936, he briefly met with Sigmund Freud. It was reported that the meeting was unpleasant.

In 1942, Fritz Perls joined the South African Army, and served as an army psychiatrist with the rank of captain until 1946.

In 1946, Fritz and Laura Perls left South Africa and moved to New York, where he worked briefly with Karen Horney and Wilhelm Reich.

He wrote his second book with the help of New York intellectual and author, Paul Goodman, who drafted the theoretical second part of the book based on Perls' hand-written notes. Along with the experiential first part, written with Ralph Hefferline, the book was entitled Gestalt Therapy and published in 1951.

Soon after publishing his second book, Fritz and Laura Perls started the first Gestalt Institute in their Manhattan apartment. Perls then began traveling throughout the United States in order to conduct Gestalt workshops and trainings.

In 1960, Fritz left Laura behind in Manhattan and moved to Los Angeles, where he practiced in conjunction with Jim Simkin. When Fritz left NYC for California, a split emerged in the Gestalt Therapy group. There were those who saw Gestalt therapy as a therapeutic approach with great potential. And there were others who saw it as a way of life. This feeling is summarized by the "Gestalt prayer" (shown at the top of this section) written by Fritz Perls.

In the 1960s, he became infamous for his public workshops at Esalen Institute in Big Sur. He also became interested in Zen during this period, and incorporated the idea of mini-satori (a brief awakening) into his practice.

In 1969, Perls left Esalen and started a Gestalt community at Lake Cowichan on Vancouver Island, Canada.

Fritz Perls died of heart failure on March 14, 1970, after undergoing heart surgery at the Louis A. Weiss Memorial Hospital.

Gestalt therapy reached its peak around the late 1970s and early 1980s and has since declined in popularity. Perls' Gestalt therapy is still functioning in Esalen at Big Sur. Many of Fritz and Laura Perls' students have also continued the development and application of Gestalt Therapy. Notable students include Richard Bandler and John Grinder, the co-founders of NLP, as well as Claudio Naranjo, Fritz Perls' apprentice.

Chapter 3: Attitude is Everything

The NLP Attitude

If you were to ask Richard Bandler, the co-founder of NLP, "What is NLP?", this is what he would say: *NLP is an attitude, backed by a methodology, that leaves behind a trail of techniques.*

It's important to note that the word "attitude" comes first. This is what many people seem to miss when it comes to understanding NLP. Many people focus on the techniques and the language patterns, but without the right attitude, none of that stuff will work for you.

Here are a few ideas you should consider when it comes to developing the right attitude:

Be purposive - act from intention.

Most people go through life with no real aim or direction. They don't expect much out of life, and as a result, they don't get much. If you wish to adopt an NLP attitude, then from this day forward, you must act with purpose. Don't be random, sporadic or unpredictable in how you act. Random results cannot be replicated, even if the result is favorable.

This is why NLP is both an art and a science. It is an art because each person brings his own unique style to NLP. It is a science because there's a specific methodology of how you go about using it.

Gandhi was a famous figure back in the day who built a large following because he acted from purpose. His purpose was to liberate India and because he stuck to that purpose, he was able to succeed in doing so.

Professionalism gets results.

People like to know they're dealing with a professional. A professional tends to have a certain air about them. They know exactly what they're doing and they know how to inspire confidence in other people.

Here's a useful definition of professionalism: "the combination of all the qualities that are connected with trained and skilled people."

Let's say you needed heart surgery and you had to choose between 2 surgeons. The first surgeon had a casual, laid-back look, and didn't seem too sure of himself. In fact, he had just gotten out of medical school a few years ago and only has a few surgeries under his belt.

Then, there's the other surgeon who looks well-dressed and has a certain look of confidence in his eye. He has been in the field for over 10 years and has dozens of surgeries under his belt. If you had to pick one, you would probably go with the professional-looking surgeon with more experience.

CHAPTER 3: ATTITUDE IS EVERYTHING

In almost every aspect of our lives, if we had to choose between the amateur and the professional, the professional wins every time. And being professional isn't just about having experience. And it isn't just about being confident. It's the sum total of experience, confidence, and overall appearance that distinguishes someone as being a professional.

Don't get too hung up on yourself if you don't have the skill just yet. That will come with time. In the meantime, carry yourself as if you already have the skills you want and you'll start to get them.

Here are a few more points to keep in mind in regards to being a professional:

- Have a positive attitude – Nobody likes a downer. Keep your head up and keep moving forward.
- Be reliable – Be the kind of person that other people can depend on.
- Take ownership – If you're responsible for something, accept what comes with it, both the good and the bad.
- Become mission-oriented – Focus on serving a higher purpose other than your material needs.
- Don't complain – If something goes wrong, spend more time on the solution than the problem. Complaining about something without doing something about it will get you nowhere.

Consider wedding competence and confidence.

Are you a confident person? For most people, it depends upon the context. If you're in a familiar environment and you know what you're doing, it's pretty easy to feel confident.

Competence, on the other hand, comes from knowing what you're doing and being able to do it well.

Keep in mind that being confident and being competent are two completely different things. However, when you use both of them together, it makes for a powerful combination. When you know what you're doing and you're certain about it, you move with a different energy. People naturally gravitate towards those who know what they're doing and are confident that they know what they're doing.

Here are a few additional things to keep in mind in regards to competence and confidence:

- **Become a good listener** - Pay attention to what the other person is saying. It will provide you the information you need to respond thoughtfully.
- **Ask the right questions** - If you're unsure about how to do something, asking the right questions will put you on the fast track towards gaining mental clarity.
- **Visualize yourself as the person you want to be** - See yourself in your mind's eye as a competent and confident person and you'll begin to live into that reality.
- **Face your fears** - Taking your fears head-on is one of the fastest ways to build confidence. Resist the urge to run away from them.

Be willing to experiment and try new things.

A wise person once said, insanity is doing the same thing over and over again, and expecting different results. Think outside of the box and you'll be surprised at what you come up with.

Be fascinated and curious.

When we were kids, it was easy to be fascinated in everything. We were young and impressionable. Everything seemed like a miracle and each day was like the beginning of a new adventure. As we got older, we began to lose our sense of wonder. And now as adults, most of us are stuck in the day-to-day grind, with no end in sight.

Sometimes, you gotta stop for a second and smell the roses. Pretend that you're a child and see the wonder and beauty in everything around you. Remember that each person you meet has a rich inner experience just like you. They have thoughts, feelings, desires, and fears, just like you.

Getting curious about the people around you will serve you well as an NLP Practitioner.

Flexibility – Be Outrageous or crazy

In order to get a different result, we have to be willing to take a different action. This may mean stepping outside our comfort zone of how we normally act. More often than not, we get stuck in the same behavioral patterns and wonder why things in our life aren't changing.

View life as a challenge

It doesn't matter if you're rich or poor, everyone has problems. The problem is rarely the "problem", but how we look at it. How can the same event happen to 2 different people and produce 2 different responses?

The answer is in how you perceive and respond to the event. If you perceive the event as a minor setback, it will be a lot easier for you to find a way to overcome it than if you thought of it as something catastrophic.

You might be thinking, "this sounds an awful lot like wishful thinking. You can't think your way into a better situation." Thinking, by itself, doesn't produce results. But, the right thinking, with the right action, will.

Whenever you get hit with something unexpected, don't immediately think of it as something bad. Instead, try to have fun with it. Look at it as something that you can overcome. If you're having trouble with that, then think about other times when you've overcome tough situations. If you've overcome challenges before, then it's very likely that you'll do it again.

See every challenge as an opportunity to better yourself. It might call upon a skill that you're already good at, or it might poke at a weakness that needs to be addressed. Whatever the case may be, don't let it get you down. You are bigger and better than any challenge that comes your way.

Use common sense

Take calculated risks and don't be outrageous to the point where you end up hurting yourself or someone else.

Always act from integrity.

In the dictionary, integrity is defined as having strong moral principles. You need to condition yourself to do the right thing without even thinking about it. This will put you on a level above mortal men. Most people are willing to take the easy way out if they think they can get away with it.

Let's say you have two employees that work at a fast food job. One person has integrity, and the other person doesn't. One day, the person with integrity finds a wallet that was left behind by one of the diners. Without thinking twice, he immediately lets his manager know and makes sure the wallet is kept in a safe place until the owner returns.

If the person without integrity were to find the wallet, he might not tell anyone about it. Or, he might check to see if there's any money in the wallet, and give himself a "reward" for finding it.

* * *

Elements of Attitude

The elements of attitude can be broken up into the 12 C's, 12 E's, and 4 I's. These are the essential qualities that you need to develop and cultivate in order to master NLP and apply it successfully in your life. Let's take a look at each of them in more detail.

12 C's of Attitude

Congruency - When your words and actions correspond with one another. This means that you are authentic and consistent in your communication and behavior. You express what you truly think and feel, and you act in alignment with your values and beliefs. Congruency builds trust and rapport with yourself and others, and enhances your credibility and influence.

Competence - To possess a wide range of skill or ability. This means that you are proficient and knowledgeable in the areas that are relevant to your goals and interests. You are always learning and improving your skills, and you seek feedback and guidance from others who are more experienced or skilled than you. Competence gives you confidence and flexibility in dealing with various situations and challenges.

Confidence - Belief in the effectiveness of one's own ability. This means that you have a positive and realistic self-image, and you trust your own judgment and capabilities. You are not afraid to take risks and try new things, and you are resilient and optimistic in the face of difficulties and setbacks. Confidence allows you to pursue your dreams and aspirations, and to inspire and motivate others to do the same.

Creativity - The ability to create meaningful new forms. This means that you are imaginative and original in your thinking and expression. You are open to new ideas and perspectives, and you can combine and transform existing elements into novel and useful solutions. Creativity enables you to overcome obstacles and find opportunities in any situation, and to add value and beauty to the world.

CHAPTER 3: ATTITUDE IS EVERYTHING

Concern - Regard for or interest in someone or something. This means that you are attentive and curious about the people and things around you. You show empathy and compassion for others, and you seek to understand their needs and feelings. You are also interested in the topics and issues that matter to you, and you seek to learn more and expand your knowledge. Concern fosters connection and collaboration with others, and stimulates your growth and development.

Care - Close attention, as in doing something well or avoiding harm. This means that you are diligent and conscientious in your actions and decisions. You pay attention to the details and quality of your work, and you strive to achieve excellence and satisfaction. You also take care of yourself and others, and you avoid causing or experiencing harm or suffering. Care enhances your performance and productivity, and promotes your well-being and happiness.

Commitment - The state of being emotionally or intellectually devoted, as to a belief, a course of action, or another person. This means that you are loyal and dedicated to your values and goals, and you are willing to invest your time and energy to achieve them. You are also faithful and supportive to the people and causes that you care about, and you honor your promises and obligations. Commitment strengthens your resolve and persistence, and builds your reputation and trustworthiness.

Curiosity - A desire to know or learn. This means that you are eager and enthusiastic to explore and discover new things. You ask questions and seek answers, and you challenge your assumptions and beliefs. You are also open-minded and receptive to feedback and criticism, and you learn from your mistakes and failures. Curiosity fuels your passion and interest, and increases your intelligence and wisdom.

Choice - The opportunity or power of choosing. This means that you are aware and responsible for your decisions and actions, and you accept the consequences of them. You are also proactive and intentional in creating and selecting the options that are available to you, and you do not let others or circumstances dictate your choices. Choice empowers you to shape your own destiny, and to exercise your freedom and autonomy.

Challenge - A test of one's abilities or resources in a demanding but stimulating undertaking. This means that you are willing and able to face and overcome difficulties and obstacles that stand in your way. You are also eager and ready to take on new and exciting tasks and projects that stretch your limits and potential. Challenge motivates you to improve and excel, and to achieve your goals and aspirations.

Clarity - Clearness of thought or style. This means that you are able to think and communicate effectively and efficiently. You have a clear and focused mind, and you can organize and express your thoughts and ideas in a logical and coherent manner. You are also able to articulate and convey your message and intention in a simple and concise way. Clarity enhances your understanding and comprehension, and improves your persuasion and influence.

Consequences - Something that logically or naturally follows from an action or condition. This means that you are aware and mindful of the impact and implications of your actions and decisions, both for yourself and others. You are also able to anticipate and evaluate the possible outcomes and results of your choices, and you can adjust and adapt accordingly. Consequences help you to make better and smarter decisions, and to achieve better and more desirable results.

CHAPTER 3: ATTITUDE IS EVERYTHING

The 12 E's of Attitude

Excellence - The state or quality of excelling or being exceptionally good. Excellence is not a fixed standard, but a dynamic process of improvement and learning. It's not about being perfect, but about being the best version of yourself.

Excitement - The feeling of lively and cheerful joy. Excitement is the fuel that drives you to pursue your dreams and passions. It's the emotion that makes you feel alive and energized and the spark that ignites your creativity and curiosity.

Envision - Being able to use your imagination and senses to create and hold a clear and compelling vision of what you want to achieve. It's the ability to transform your thoughts into reality.

Energize - The state of being fully charged and ready to take action. It is the effect of having a positive and optimistic mindset and the result of taking care of your physical, mental, and emotional well-being.

Enable - The attitude of empowering yourself and others to overcome challenges and achieve goals. You provide the necessary resources and support to facilitate growth and change. It's the habit of giving and receiving feedback and encouragement.

Ecology - The dynamic balance of elements in any system. A concern for the overall relationship between a being and its environment. This is the principle of respecting and harmonizing with yourself, others, and nature. It's the value of considering the consequences and impact of your actions and decisions.

Entertain - To hold the attention of pleasantly or agreeably. This is the art of making your communication engaging and enjoyable. It's the strategy of using humor, stories, and metaphors to convey your message and connect with your audience.

Enlightenment - The process of gaining insight and understanding of yourself and the world. It is the state of being aware and conscious of your thoughts, feelings, and actions. It is the experience of transcending your limitations and expanding your potential.

Expectation - This is the mindset of anticipating and attracting positive outcomes. It's the belief that you deserve and can achieve what you want. It's the force that shapes your reality and influences your behavior.

Experiment - The attitude of being open and curious to explore new possibilities and opportunities. It is the action of testing and applying different methods and strategies to find what works best for you. It is the habit of learning from your failures and successes.

Ecstasy - This is the emotion that you feel when you are fully immersed and absorbed in what you are doing. It is the state that you reach when you are in flow and peak performance. It is the reward that you get when you achieve your goals and fulfill your purpose.

Eliminate Seriousness - This is the attitude of not taking yourself or life too seriously. It's the action of letting go of stress and worry and embracing playfulness and spontaneity. It's the habit of finding joy and gratitude in every moment.

The 4 I's of Attitude

Integrity - the quality of being honest and having strong moral principles. It means that you are congruent with your words and actions, and that you respect yourself and others. Integrity allows you to build trust and rapport with yourself and others, and to align your conscious and unconscious mind. When you have integrity, you are authentic and consistent, and you can access your inner resources more easily.

Impeccability - The state of being free from fault or error. It means that you strive for excellence and accuracy in everything you do, and that you take responsibility for your results. Impeccability is important because it enables you to set high standards and achieve your desired outcomes. When you are impeccable, you are precise and effective, and you can learn from your feedback and improve your performance.

Integration - The process of bringing separate things together in a cohesive unity. It means that you harmonize your thoughts, feelings, and behaviors, and that you integrate different aspects of yourself and others. Integration is vital because it allows you to create balance and synergy in your life. When you are integrated, you are flexible and adaptable, and you can leverage your diversity and creativity.

Intentionality - The fact of being deliberate and purposeful. It means that you have a clear vision and direction, and that you act with focus and commitment. Intentionality is crucial because it empowers you to create your own reality and achieve your goals. When you are intentional, you are proactive and motivated, and you can influence yourself and others.

There are many facets to consider when it comes to developing the NLP Attitude. My suggestion to you would be to pick 2 or 3 of these traits and do the best you can to integrate them into your daily life. Start mastering them little by little, and over time, you'll have fully adopted the NLP attitude.

Chapter 4: How We Think & Experience

NLP Communication Model

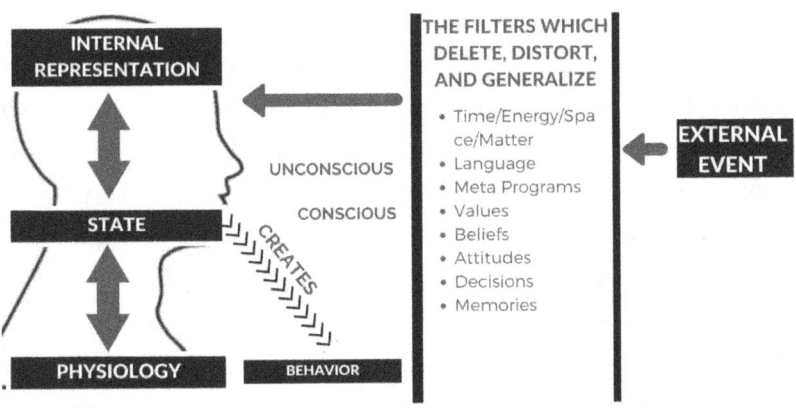

The NLP Communication Model explains how experience gets transferred and encoded from the external environment to the internal environment.

First, an external event happens in the outside environment. The external event then gets picked up our sensory receptors, which correspond to the 5 representational systems, Visual, Auditory, Kinesthetic, etc. These are the modalities through which we perceive the world and create sensory-based representations of our experience.

Our internal processing filters delete, distort, and generalize the event. Various internal processing filters shape our internal representation.

First, there's Time/Space/Energy/Matter. These are the essential building blocks of reality that all experience must go through. They determine how we locate ourselves and the event in relation to the physical world and its properties. For example, we may perceive the event as happening in the past, present, or future, or as being near or far, big or small, fast or slow, etc.

Next, there's language. Language is the primary tool for communication and meaning-making, but it also limits and shapes our perception of reality. The way we label, describe, and interpret the event influences how we feel and act about it. For example, we may use positive or negative words, metaphors or literal expressions, questions or statements, etc.

Our memories and decisions also have a profound effect on how we perceive things. They are the stored representations of our past experiences and the choices we made based on them. They form the basis of our learning and behavior patterns, and they also influence how we anticipate and evaluate the event. For example, we may recall similar or contrasting events, associate the event with positive or negative outcomes, or compare the event with our expectations or goals, etc.

There's also our beliefs, values, attitudes, and Meta-Programs, which we'll be talking about in a separate section. These are the deeper and more abstract filters that govern our perception of reality and ourselves. They are the assumptions, criteria, preferences, and tendencies that we have about the world and how it works. They determine what we consider to be true, important, desirable, and possible, and they also influence how we motivate, persuade, and influence ourselves and others. For example, we may believe that the event is good or bad, valuable or worthless, easy or hard, etc.

Our internal representations of the event affect our state, which also affects our physiology, and vice-versa. Our state is the combination of our thoughts, feelings, and bodily sensations that we experience at any given moment. It is the result of our internal processing of the event, and it also influences how we process the event further.

Our physiology is the physical manifestation of our state, such as our posture, breathing, facial expression, etc. It is the outward expression of our state, and it also influences how we feel and think. For example, we may feel happy or sad, confident or nervous, relaxed or tense, etc.

Our state goes on to affect our behaviors. Our behaviors are the actions and reactions that we perform in response to the event. They are the outcome of our state, and they also influence our state and the event itself. Our behaviors can be verbal or non-verbal, conscious or unconscious, intentional or accidental, etc. They are the ways we express ourselves and interact with the world.

In conclusion, everything is interconnected, from the external to internal. The NLP Communication Model shows us how we create our subjective experience of reality, and how we can change it by changing any of the elements involved. By becoming aware of our internal processing and its effects, we can enhance our communication and personal development.

* * *

Neurological Levels

Neurological Levels was created by Robert Dilts and Todd Epstein, two prominent NLP Trainers. We can use it to organize our thoughts and determine where our difficulties lie. They also show us how we can change ourselves and our situations by moving up the levels of awareness and understanding.

The neurological levels are 6 in total, and they form a hierarchy from bottom to top. The lower levels are more concrete and observable, while the higher levels are more abstract and conceptual.

At the bottom, we have environment, which is the lowest level in the hierarchy. It refers to all the external conditions that affect us in our life. These include physical factors such as weather, location, time zone, etc., as well as social factors such as family, friends, colleagues, culture, etc. We experience the environment with our senses: sight, hearing, touch, smell, taste. The main question to ask at this level is: "What context does this behavior occur?" For example: "Where did this happen?" or "What are the contributing factors?"

Next, is the level of behavior, which includes all externally perceived actions and reactions that we display or observe in ourselves or others. These include words (spoken or written), gestures (facial expressions or body movements), movements (walking or sitting), breathing (rate or rhythm), etc. Behavior can be described with sense-specific terms: what we see (e.g., red), hear (e.g., loud), and feel (e.g., hot). The main question to ask at this level is: "What am I able to do?" For example: "Can I speak another language?" or "Can I play an instrument?"

Capabilities deals with the cognitive and emotional processes that we go through to make a certain behavior possible. These include skills (knowledge or expertise), abilities (potential or capacity), talents (natural aptitude or flair), strengths (positive qualities or resources), weaknesses (negative limitations or challenges). Capabilities can be described with sense-specific terms: what we know (e.g., history), what we can do (e.g., solve problems), what we have done before (e.g., won awards), what we like about ourselves (e.g., confident), what we need to improve on (e.g., patient). The main question to ask at this level is: "How?" For example: "How do I learn a new skill?" or "How do I cope with stress?"

Values and Beliefs are the inner criteria that underlie the actions we do. They reflect what we consider to be right, true, important, or desirable. They shape our worldview, our goals, our preferences, and our judgments. Values are general principles or standards that guide our decisions and actions. Beliefs are specific convictions or assumptions that support our values. Values and beliefs can be described with abstract terms: what we value (e.g., honesty), what we believe (e.g., God exists). The main question to ask at this level is: "Why?" For example: "Why do I value honesty?" or "Why do I believe God exists?"

The next level is identity, which deals with our self-image, our sense of who we are. It includes all the ideas that we construct about ourselves, our behavior, our abilities, our beliefs, and so on. It is the central model of our overall personality. Identity can be described with abstract terms: who I am (e.g., a teacher), what I do (e.g., write books), how I feel (e.g., happy). The main question to ask at this level is: "Who am I?" For example: "Who am I as a writer?" or "Who am I as a person?"

Mission is generally regarded as the highest level of the model. Your mission could be philosophical, political, social, or religious, to name a few. This level guides and shapes our life and give our existence a foundation. It answers the big questions like "Why are we here?" or "what is the meaning of life?"

* * *

NLP Representational Systems

The 5 main NLP Representation Systems are Visual (sight), Auditory (hearing), Kinesthetic (bodily sensations), Olfactory (smelling), and Gustatory (tasting). Out of those 5, Visual, Auditory, and Kinesthetic are considered the main ones. Other representational systems include Auditory-Digital (self-talk), Auditory-tonal (sounds and music), Kinesthetic-visceral (gut sensations), Kinesthetic-tactile (touch), and Kinesthetic-meta (emotions).

Each representation system has a 3-part network: Input, Representation/Processing, and output. The first stage involves gathering information from the environment. The second stage involves mapping the environment and establishing behavioral strategies such as learning, thinking, deciding, etc. The final stage, or output, is the "causal transform of the representational mapping process", as described in NLP Vol. 1.

All output is behavior, and behavior is activity within any of the representational system complex at any of the stages. In other words, seeing, feeling, and hearing, are all forms of behavior.

Representations by themselves are meaningless. We can only determine the significance of a representation system by how it functions in the context of a strategy in a human's behavior. Representations can serve as a limitation or resource, depending on how it's being used. For example, if you were to take an artist and a schizophrenic and have both of them engage in visualization, the visualization would be far more productive for the artist than it would be for the schizophrenic.

General Characteristics Based on Primary Rep System

As human beings grow from infants to adulthood, we tend to prefer one representational system over all the others.

Your primary representation system plays a significant role when it comes to your personality type. Studies have also shown a direct correlation between an individual's primary representation system and certain physiological and psychological characteristics.

Here's a brief overview of each one:

Visual People

Visual people tend to stand or sit with their bodies erect and their eyes looking upward. They tend to have shallow breathing and it's high in the chest. They are easily distracted by noise. They also learn and memorize things by seeing pictures. They make up about 60 percent of the population.

Auditory People

Auditory people tend to move their eyes from side to side. They have regular and rhythmic breathing in the middle of their chest. They tend to be very good with words and learn best by listening. They also tend to lean forward while talking. They make up 20 percent of the population.

Kinesthetic People

Kinesthetic people often use words that indicate motion, sensation, and/or action. They breathe deep into the stomach. They tend to move slowly. They enjoy closeness with other people. They feel deeply and love deeply. They make up about 20 percent of the population.

Auditory-Digital People

These people operate at a meta-level of awareness above the sensory level of VAK. They tend to come off like a "computer". They have a monotone voice and their lips are thin and light.

Building Rapport With Others

One of the best ways to get into rapport with someone is to use words that match their primary representation system. You can get an idea of what someone's primary representation system is by listening to the kinds of predicates they use.

Here are some examples based on each representation system:

Visual: appear, glow, graphic, sparkle, vivid, reflect, colorful, cloudy

Auditory: harmonize, explain, echo, inquire, complain, discuss, talk, request

Kinesthetic: grapple, exciting, smooth, run, comfortable, warm, work

Olfactory/Gustatory: bitter, spicy, sweet, stale, savor, odor, fresh

Here are some predicate phrases you can listen out for as well:

Visual: paint a picture, eye to eye, bird's eye view, beyond a shadow of a doubt, see to it

Auditory: loud and clear, unheard of, rings a bell, hold your tongue, manner of speaking

Kinesthetic: hand in hand, tap into, turn around, pain-in-the-neck, pull some strings

NLP Sub-modalities

The brain represents all experience using modalities and the quality or properties of those modalities. These qualities or properties are known as sub-modalities. Sub-modalities allow us to speak with greater precision about the content of our thoughts. We can make finer distinctions in our internal representations and these distinctions are what create the messages and commands for how to feel and respond.

This is why it's a common NLP saying that "sub-modalities drive behavior".

Sub-modalities can be broken down into 2 types: digital and analog sub-modalities. Digital sub-modalities are either on or off. There's no in-between. For example, color or black-and-white would be considered a digital sub-modality. A picture or movie is another example of a digital sub-modality. Analog sub-modalities exist along a continuum. Examples include loudness, brightness, blurriness, and contrast.

When certain sub-modalities get altered, they may alter other sub-modalities as well like a chain reaction. We call these sub-modalities "driver sub-modalities".

Going Meta

To detect the specific qualities and attributes of a particular modality, you have to go "meta" or above the internal representation.

Human beings have 2 levels of thought. The first level of thought is known as the primary state. The primary state is our everyday states of consciousness where we experience thoughts-and-feelings about the outside world. The second level is known as the meta-states. This is where we have thoughts about our thoughts, feelings about feelings, and states about states. We'll discuss more about Meta-States in a later chapter.

At the second level, this is where our thoughts and emotions relate to and about the world "inside" ourselves. Our beliefs exist on this level as well, which is why it's often insufficient to change beliefs by shifting sub-modalities, which operate at a lower level.

To believe in something, you have to say "yes" to the representation.

To disbelieve in something, you have to say "no" to the representation.

In order to turn a thought into a belief, or a belief into just a mere thought, you have to move to a meta-level and either confirm or disconfirm the thought. We need to shift the sub-modalities that affect the saying of "yes" or "no" to the representation.

Think about an experience, then think about how you THINK about the experience.

Is it bright or dark?

Is it a picture or a movie?

Is it blurry or in focus?

By asking these kinds of questions, you're able to put yourself into a higher frame of mind where you can start altering the qualities of your internal representations.

* * *

Eye-Accessing Cues

Eye-accessing cues are involuntary eye movements that indicate which representational system someone is using at any given moment. They are called cues because they can give us a hint into what someone is thinking, feeling, or remembering. Eye-accessing cues were discovered by Richard Bandler and John Grinder, the co-founders of NLP, after observing thousands of people from different backgrounds and cultures. They found that there was a consistent pattern of eye movements that correlated with different types of mental processes.

However, eye movements do not cause internal experience, they only reflect it. This means that you cannot change someone's thoughts or feelings by making them move their eyes in a certain way. But you can use your own eye movements to access different representational systems and enhance your creativity, memory, and learning. You can also use eye-accessing cues to build rapport with others, by matching their eye movements and using the same representational system as they do.

There are two types of eye patterns: normally organized and reversed organized. Normally organized people move their eyes in the same direction as shown in the diagram below. Reversed organized people move their eyes in the opposite direction. About 80% of the population is normally organized, and the remaining 20% is reversed organized. This can vary depending on factors such as handedness, brain dominance, and cultural background.

Here's a common diagram of eye-accessing cues:

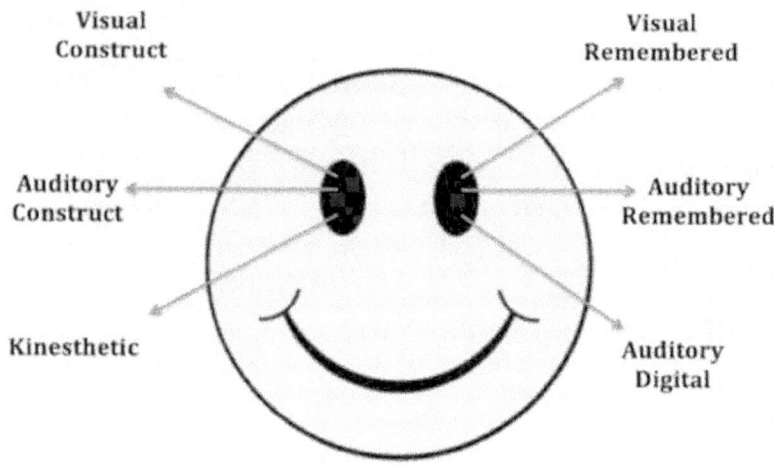

Figure 2. EAC (Eye Accessing Cues) (Palande, 2015. With permission)

This diagram shows the eye movements of a person that's normally organized. This is from the perspective of looking directly at a person. The eye movements are divided into 3 categories: upper, middle, and lower. The upper category indicates visual processing, the middle category is auditory processing, and the lower category is split between kinesthetic and auditory-digital, or self-talk. The left direction (from the other person's perspective) indicates remembered or recalled information while the right side is constructed or imagined information.

There's a quick and easy way to tell if someone is normally organized or reversed organized, based on which wrist they wear their watch. If they wear their watch on their left wrist, then they are normally organized. If they wear their watch on their right wrist, then they're reversed organized. This is because time is an auditory-digital sense and people tend to wear their watch where they access auditory-digital.

* * *

Strategies 101

A strategy is a specific sequence of internal and external experiences that lead to a desired outcome. In other words, a strategy is the how of doing something.

We use strategies for everything we do, whether consciously or unconsciously. Some examples of common strategies are:

- How we fall in love
- How we learn new skills
- How we motivate ourselves
- How we make decisions
- How we create wealth
- How we have fun

Understanding and changing our strategies can help us improve our performance, achieve our goals, and enhance our well-being.

To identify and modify a strategy, we need to know its two components:

elements and sequence. The elements are the representational systems that we use to process information: Visual, Auditory, Kinesthetic, Olfactory, Gustatory, and Auditory-Digital. These are also known as VAKOGAD for short.

Each representational system can be either internal or external, depending on whether we generate it in our mind or perceive it from the environment. For example, we can have an internal visual image of a sunset, or an external visual perception of a painting.

Internal representations can also be either constructed or remembered, depending on whether we create them from scratch or recall them from memory. For example, we can have an internal auditory constructed sound of a song we never heard before, or an internal auditory remembered sound of a song we know well.

Auditory-Digital, also known as self-talk, is a special element that represents our internal dialogue and logical thinking. Unlike the other representational systems, there is no distinction between internal and external, or constructed and remembered, for Auditory-Digital.

The sequence is the order in which we use the elements to form a strategy. The sequence determines the effectiveness and quality of the strategy. For example, a strategy for learning a new language might involve:

- Visual external: looking at the words and symbols
- Auditory external: listening to the pronunciation and intonation
- Auditory-Digital: analyzing the grammar and syntax
- Kinesthetic internal: feeling the emotion and meaning

- Auditory internal remembered: repeating the words and phrases

Strategies play a critical role in modeling other people. Modeling is the process of replicating the excellence of someone else by mapping their cognitive sequence. By using the same strategy as a successful person, we can achieve similar results. For example, if we want to model a great speaker, we can elicit their strategy for preparing and delivering a speech, and then apply it to our own situation.

* * *

Time-lines

One of the most fascinating aspects of NLP is how it reveals the different ways that people perceive and relate to time. Time isn't just a linear sequence of events, but a subjective experience that can vary from person to person. In this section, we'll explore the concept of time-lines, how they affect our behavior and emotions, and how we can use them to enhance our personal and professional lives.

What are time-lines?

Time-lines are the mental images or representations that we have of our past, present, and future. They are like a movie that plays in our mind, showing us where we have been, where we are, and where we are going. Time-lines are not fixed or objective, but rather flexible and influenced by our beliefs, values, memories, and expectations.

How do we experience time-lines?

There are many ways that people can experience their time-lines, but the two most common types are left to right and behind to front. These types are also known as through time and in time, respectively.

Left to right or through time means that you see your time-line in front of you, horizontally, from left to right. The left side usually represents the past, the right side the future, and the center the present. You can easily access any point on your time-line by moving your eyes or your head. You are aware of the passage of time and can plan ahead and manage your schedule effectively. You tend to be punctual, organized, and goal-oriented.

Behind to front or in time means that you see your time-line passing through you, vertically, from behind to front. The back side represents the past, the front side the future, and the middle the present. You can access any point on your time-line by turning around or moving your body. You are immersed in the present moment and can enjoy the here and now. You tend to be spontaneous, flexible, and creative.

Of course, these are not the only ways to experience time-lines. Some people may see their time-line from below to above, from right to left, or in a circular or spiral shape. Some people may have more than one time-line, or switch between different types depending on the context. The important thing is to recognize your own preferred way of experiencing time and how it affects your life.

How can we use time-lines?

CHAPTER 4: HOW WE THINK & EXPERIENCE

Time-lines are powerful tools that we can use to change our emotional states, achieve our goals, and heal our past. Here are some examples of how we can use time-lines:

- To access positive emotions and resources: We can revisit a moment in our past when we felt a certain emotion or quality, such as confidence, joy, or love, and bring it back to the present. We can also project ourselves into the future and imagine how we would feel when we achieve a desired outcome, such as getting a promotion, finding a partner, or traveling the world. By doing this, we can create a positive anchor that we can activate whenever we need it.

- To clear negative emotions and beliefs: We can identify a moment in our past when we felt a negative emotion or developed a limiting belief, such as fear, anger, or guilt, and change it. We can do this by changing the sub-modalities of our time-line, such as the size, color, brightness, distance, or sound of the image. We can also reframe the meaning of the event, or add new resources and perspectives. By doing this, we can release the emotional charge and create a new association that empowers us.

- To set and achieve goals: We can create a clear and compelling vision of our future and place it on our time-line. We can make sure that our vision is aligned with our values, ecology, and identity. We can also break down our vision into smaller steps and milestones, and place them on our time-line as well. By doing this, we can create a roadmap that guides us and motivates us to take action.

These are just some of the ways that we can use time-lines to enhance our lives. In a good NLP certification course, you can learn more about the theory and practice of time-lines, and how to apply them in different contexts and situations. Time-lines are a fascinating and powerful aspect of NLP that can help you understand yourself and others better, and create the life that you want.

* * *

Hierarchy of Ideas

CHAPTER 4: HOW WE THINK & EXPERIENCE

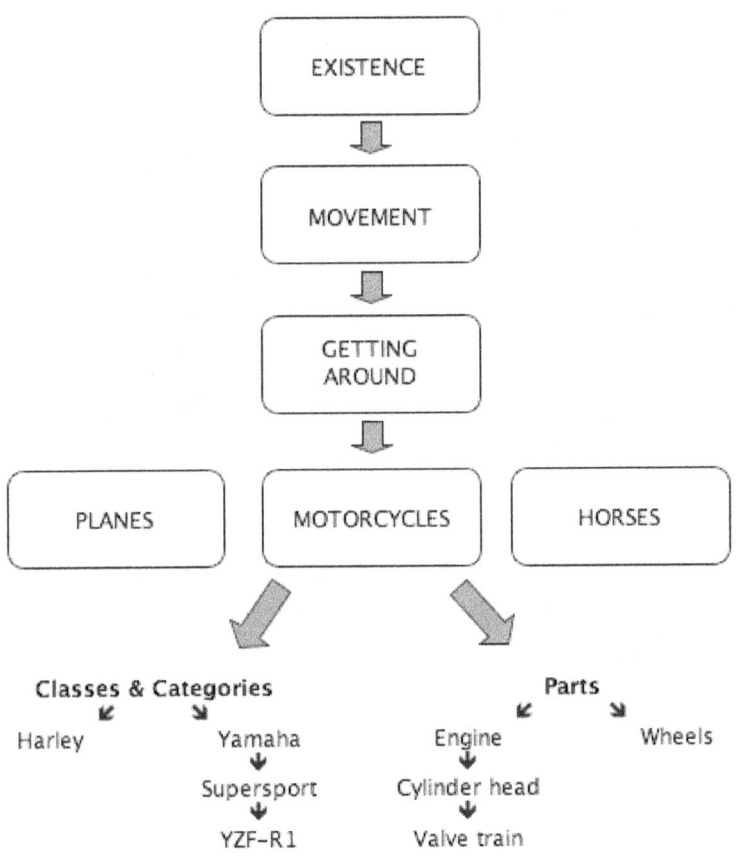

Credit: Practical NLP Podcast

The hierarchy of ideas is a powerful tool in Neuro-linguistic Programming (NLP) that helps us to communicate more effectively and persuasively. It is based on the principle that different levels of abstraction can have different effects on our thinking and behavior.

The hierarchy of ideas can be visualized as a pyramid, where the top represents the most abstract and general concepts, and the bottom represents the most concrete and specific details. For example, at the top of the pyramid, we might have the concept of "life", and at the bottom, we might have the name of a specific person.

We can move up and down the hierarchy of ideas by using a technique called chunking. Chunking is the process of grouping or dividing information into smaller or larger units, depending on our purpose. Chunking up means moving to a higher level of abstraction, where we focus on the similarities and the big picture. Chunking down means moving to a lower level of specificity, where we focus on the differences and the details.

Chunking up and down can have different effects on our mental state and our ability to influence others. By chunking up, we can create a sense of connection, rapport, and agreement with others, as well as access more creative and resourceful states of mind. By chunking down, we can create a sense of clarity, realism, and action, as well as challenge and test the validity of our assumptions and beliefs.

There is also another type of chunking, called lateral chunking, where we move to the same level of abstraction, but in a different direction. Lateral chunking allows us to explore alternative perspectives, options, and possibilities, without changing the level of detail or generality. For example, if we are talking about cars, we can chunk laterally by considering different types, models, or brands of cars.

To chunk up, we can use questions like "What is this an example of?", "What is the purpose of this?", or "What is the higher intention behind this?". To chunk down, we can use questions like "What is an example of this?", "How can we achieve this?", or "What are the steps involved in this?". To chunk laterally, we can use questions like "What else is like this?", "What are some other ways to do this?", or "What are some other outcomes of this?".

Mastering the hierarchy of ideas and the skill of chunking can help us to become more flexible and effective communicators and influencers. By knowing how to move up and down the hierarchy of ideas, we can match and mismatch the level of abstraction of our listeners, depending on whether we want to create rapport or contrast. By knowing how to chunk laterally, we can expand our range of choices and solutions, and avoid getting stuck in a limited or biased view. The hierarchy of ideas is one of the most useful and versatile tools in NLP, and it can help us to achieve our goals and outcomes in any context.

* * *

NLP Frames

In NLP, a frame is a context or perspective that we use to interpret and understand a situation, an event, or a person. Frames are important because they determine the meaning that we assign to something, and the meaning affects our emotions, beliefs, and actions.

For example, imagine that you are walking down the street and you see a stranger smiling at you. Depending on your frame, you might interpret this as a friendly gesture, a flirtatious signal, a sarcastic remark, or a sign of insanity. Each frame will create a different meaning, and a different emotional response in you.

The good news is that frames are not fixed or permanent. We can change our frames, and by doing so, we can change the meaning and the emotional impact of any situation. This gives us more flexibility, choice, and control over our lives.

In this section, I will introduce you to 6 useful frames that you can apply to any situation, especially when you want to achieve a specific outcome, or when you face a challenge or a problem. These frames are: Ecology Frame, Contrasts Frame, Evidence Frame, Outcome Frame, Discovery Frame, and Backtrack Frame.

Let's look at each frame in more detail.

Ecology Frame

The Ecology Frame helps you to consider the consequences and implications of your outcome, and how it affects other aspects of your life that are important to you. It helps you to ensure that your outcome is aligned with your values, beliefs, and identity, and that it does not create any conflicts or trade-offs with other outcomes that you want.

To use the Ecology Frame, ask yourself questions like:

- How will achieving this outcome affect my life in the short-term and the long-term?
- How will achieving this outcome affect the people around me, such as my family, friends, colleagues, or customers?

- Is this outcome consistent with who I am and what I stand for?
- Is this outcome worth the time, energy, and resources that I will invest in it?
- What are the potential risks or drawbacks of achieving this outcome?

The Ecology Frame helps you to evaluate your outcome from a holistic and systemic perspective, and to avoid any unwanted or harmful side effects. It also helps you to enhance your outcome by finding ways to make it more beneficial and satisfying for yourself and others.

Contrasts Frame

The Contrasts Frame helps you to notice the differences that make a difference. It helps you to compare and contrast different situations, events, or people, and to identify the factors that make them unique, special, or effective.

The Contrasts Frame is the foundation of NLP, as it is based on the principle of modeling. Modeling is the process of observing and replicating the excellence of others, by discovering the strategies, techniques, and mindsets that they use to achieve outstanding results.

To use the Contrasts Frame, ask yourself questions like:

- What are the differences between this situation and that situation?
- What are the differences between this person and that person?
- What are the differences between what I am doing and what they are doing?

- What are the differences between what works and what doesn't work?
- What are the differences between what I want and what I don't want?

The Contrasts Frame helps you to learn from the best, by finding out what makes them different and better than the rest. It also helps you to improve your own performance, by adopting the strategies, techniques, and mindsets that work for them.

Evidence Frame

The Evidence Frame helps you to define and measure your outcome, and to know when you have achieved it. It helps you to specify the criteria and indicators that will tell you that you have reached your desired state, and to verify your progress and results.

To use the Evidence Frame, ask yourself questions like:

- How will I know that I have achieved my outcome?
- What will I see, hear, and feel when I achieve my outcome?
- How will I measure my outcome, both quantitatively and qualitatively?
- What are the signs and signals that will show me that I am on track or off track?
- How will I celebrate and reward myself when I achieve my outcome?

The Evidence Frame helps you to clarify your outcome, by making it more concrete, observable, and testable. It also helps you to motivate yourself, by giving you feedback and recognition for your achievements.

Outcome Frame

The Outcome Frame helps you to focus on your desired state, and to plan and take action to achieve it. It helps you to visualize and describe your outcome in positive and compelling terms and to identify and implement the steps, resources, and strategies that will lead you to it.

To use the Outcome Frame, ask yourself questions like:

- What do I want to achieve?
- Why do I want to achieve it?
- How will I achieve it?
- What are the steps that I need to take to achieve it?
- What are the resources and strategies that I need to use to achieve it?

The Outcome Frame helps you to empower yourself, by giving you a clear direction and purpose, and by enabling you to take action and make things happen. It also helps you to optimize your outcome, by finding the most effective and efficient ways to achieve it.

Note: After applying the Outcome Frame, use the Ecology Frame to ensure that your outcome is congruent and ecological.

Discovery Frame

The Discovery Frame helps you to approach any situation with an open and curious mind, and to learn from it. It helps you to suspend any judgments, expectations, or attachments to a particular outcome, and to explore and experiment with different possibilities and options.

To use the Discovery Frame, ask yourself questions like:

- What can I learn from this situation?
- What are the opportunities and challenges that this situation presents?
- What are the alternatives and variations that I can try in this situation?
- What are the effects and consequences of each option that I choose in this situation?
- What are the feedback and lessons that I can get from this situation?

The Discovery Frame helps you to enjoy the process, by making it more fun, playful, and creative. It also helps you to grow from the experience, by discovering new insights, skills, and solutions.

Backtrack Frame

The Backtrack Frame helps you to communicate effectively with others, and to build rapport and trust with them. It helps you to summarize and reflect what the other person has said, using their own words, tone, and body language. It also helps you to check for agreement and understanding of what has been said, and to resolve any misunderstandings or conflicts that may arise.

To use the Backtrack Frame, ask yourself questions like:

- What did the other person say?
- How can I repeat what they said using their own words, tone, and body language?
- How can I check if I understood them correctly, and if they understood me correctly?
- How can I acknowledge and validate their point of view, even if I disagree with it?
- How can I find a common ground and a win-win solution with them?

The Backtrack Frame helps you to listen actively and attentively, by showing that you are paying attention and that you care about what they say. It also helps you to influence positively and persuasively, by creating rapport and trust, and by finding areas of agreement and cooperation.

* * *

Meta-Programs

When it comes to understanding Meta-Programs, we're not so much interested in the content of our thoughts, behaviors, and actions. Rather, we're paying attention to the processes that govern how we think, behave, and act.

You can think of each Meta-Program as describing a wide range of "frames-of-mind". To put it another way, they are distinctions of consciousness. Every person that you come in contact with is operating from a specific frame-of-mind. That "frame-of-mind" or "program" lies above or "meta" to the thoughts, behaviors, and actions that are taking place.

Humans are made up of software and hardware, much like computers are. For us humans, our hardware includes our neurology, nervous system, brain, blood chemistry, and so on. All of these physical features play a role in shaping how we perceive things. On the software side, we have our thinking patterns, ideational categories, belief concepts, etc.

According to L. Michael Hall, to run our thoughts-and-emotions, we need a software program, so to speak, that provides instructions on how to process thoughts-and-emotions. This software provides us with the functional equivalent of an operating system. This operating system connects the hardware with the software so that the neurology of brain-and-body can input, process, and output the "information" of thoughts, ideas, beliefs, etc. This is what we refer to as Meta-Programs.

In terms of levels, our everyday thoughts and emotions operate on the primary level as the content that describes what we think-and-feel.

Above the content of our thoughts, we have other thoughts-and-feelings that operate outside of conscious awareness. These "programs" function as the sorting and perceiving mechanism that govern how we think and emote. They determine the structure of thoughts-and-feelings and direct what we sort for.

Meta-Programs trace their origin back to a woman named Leslie

Cameron-Bandler. At the time, she was working very closely with Richard Bandler, the co-founder of NLP. She had started noticing that whenever she would do "textbook" NLP, she wouldn't always get the response she was looking for.

It was while working through these "failures" with Richard that they began to create the initial list of Meta-Programs. While these distinctions were initially developed within the context of therapy, other people began to employ Meta-Programs for different uses.

For example, Roger Bailey and Ross Stewart were the first to take the Meta-Programs and apply them to a business context. Next, there was Wyatt Woodsmall, another prominent NLP Trainer, who expanded on the Meta-Programs and integrated them with the Myers-Briggs Personality Inventory. This helped to lay the groundwork for one of his best-known works, Timeline Therapy and the Basis of Personality, which he co-authored with Tad James.

Reese and Bagley came onto the scene afterward and applied Meta-Programs to profiling people and the context of selling. There are about 51 Meta-Programs in total, and you can roughly divide them into 5 categories. I say "roughly" because some of the Meta-Programs can fit into more than 1 category.

Because there are so many of them, it's useful to group them into different categories, so it doesn't become overwhelming.

Here are the 5 categories of Meta-Programs:

- Mental Meta-Programs

- Emotional Meta-Programs
- Volitional Meta-Programs
- Response Meta-Programs
- Meta Meta-Programs

Mental Meta-Programs deal with how we think, sort, and perceive things. They describe how our attention functions in terms of how it attends and processes information cognitively and what it attends.

Emotional Meta-Programs deal with emoting and somatizing. They describe how our cognitive and mental processes "emote" as it creates our emotional states of consciousness.

Volitional Meta-Programs deal with willing, choosing, and conation. This describes our operational system for deciding, opting, preferring, and focusing attention.

Response Meta-Programs deal with outputting, responding, and communication. It includes how we act, gesture, behave, etc. This implies that information processing doesn't just happen in the brain, but in our bodies as well.

Meta Meta-Programs deal with Conceptual/Semantic Realities, Identity, Self, and Time. They describe the prior "formatting" of perception that constrains consciousness.

If you'd like to dive deeper into the subject of Meta-Programs, I recommend checking out Figuring Out People: Reading People Using Meta-Programs by L. Michael Hall and Bob G. Bodenhamer.

CHAPTER 4: HOW WE THINK & EXPERIENCE

We've also published an entire course on the Meta-Programs called NLP Meta-Programs Mastery Course outlining all 51 Meta-Programs across all 5 categories.

Go to pcilinks.com/meta-programs for more information. Use the code METAPROGRAMS at checkout to get 20% off your order.

Chapter 5: NLP Modeling

Introduction

Modeling lies at the heart of NLP. It was through the process of modeling that the Milton Model and Meta Model were created.

First, Richard Bandler had modeled Fritz Perls and Virginia Satir on his own and began forming study groups on-campus at the University of California. John Grinder was an assistant professor at the time, and eventually, the 2 of them ran into each other. Both of them were fascinated by Richard's ability and wanted to formalize exactly what he was doing.

Grinder made an offer to Bandler that went something like "If you teach me what you are doing, then I will tell you what you are doing." From there, the rest is history.

The idea behind modeling is simple: You find someone who has above-average skill in a particular domain, you figure out how they do it, and you install that skill either in yourself or other people.

Modeling achieves 2 particular goals: getting a particular result and learning explicitly how to do it. Not only does the modeler benefit from learning a new skill, but the person being modeled will gain a deeper understanding of how they do what they do.

* * *

Basic Principles of Modeling

NLP Modeling Applications

According to the dictionary, a model is a "system or thing used as an example to follow or imitate." This comes close to describing the NLP modeling process. In NLP Modeling, we are creating a thing to be "followed and imitated" to achieve a specific result.

A common application of NLP modeling includes repeating or refining a performance by specifying the steps followed by elite performers or during optimal examples of the activity.

Let's take the game of chess. As of 2022, the top person in chess is a guy named Magnus Carlsen, considered to be one of the greatest chess players of all time. If you wanted to model certain chess-related skills, then Magnus would be an excellent candidate.

Modeling is flexible in the sense that you don't have to apply the skill you learned in the same context that you originally found it. You can formalize a process through modeling and apply it to a completely different context. The possibilities are nearly endless.

Levels of Modeling

When it comes to modeling effective behaviors, there are multiple levels we may need to look at. The levels of modeling mirror the Neurological Levels which we covered in Chapter 4. Each level contains 2 sub-levels (with a few exceptions) called a macro-level and a micro-level.

Environment

The first level is known as the environment. At this level, we are considering when and where the person is performing the activity. The environment determines the external opportunities and the constraints that the person must react to.

The macro-environment includes things like the general habit and social context. The micro-environment involves specific locations like an office, classroom, auditorium, etc. In addition to the environment itself, we also look at the influence the person is having on their environment.

Behavior

Behavior is specifically what the person is doing and how they're reacting in their environment. Macro-behaviors include things like general patterns, communications, and styles. Micro-behaviors include things like tasks, specific work routines, and work habits.

Capabilities

Capabilities are how a person generates behaviors in a particular context. This can be in the form of a mental map, plan, or strategy. Macro-capabilities include general strategies and skills like learning, memory, motivation, decision-making, and creativity. Micro-capabilities include things like visualization, internal self-dialogue, or how a person specifically uses their sense or cognitive capabilities during a particular behavior or task.

Beliefs and Values

Beliefs and values tell us why a person does a particular thing in a particular time and place. They help to provide reinforcement that either supports or inhibits capabilities. On a macro-level, beliefs and values relate to the type of meaning, cause-effect relations, and boundaries people place on events or perceive in the surrounding world. On a micro-level, a person's beliefs and values can relate to processes on other levels. A person may have beliefs about their environment, behavior, capabilities, etc.

Identity

We all have an identity in relation to our beliefs, capabilities, and actions, within a given environment. In other words, we need to consider the who behind the what, when, where, why, and how. In order to establish a particular role, one must have a mission within the larger system that he or she is operating.

Spiritual

In the context of NLP modeling, spiritual refers to how a person relates to the people around him such as family, colleagues, social class, culture, and so on. This is in regards to the larger system that one is a part of.

Vision

The vision is based on the spiritual level and helps to define the purpose of an individual's behaviors, abilities, beliefs, values, and identity within the larger system that he or she is a part of. This level tends to be what ties everything together and gives all the other levels their ultimate meaning.

NLP Master Trainer Robert Dilts suggests we visualize the relationship of each level as a network of generative systems that focus or converge on the identity of the individual as the core of the modeling process.

Modeling Capabilities

Most NLP modeling processes focus on the capabilities level, also known as the "how-to". Capabilities are what connect beliefs and values to specific behaviors. Without the "how", knowing what one is supposed to do and why to do it is ineffective.

Even though a strong emphasis is placed on modeling capabilities, that doesn't mean it's the only level that is looked at. Creating an effective model is often a gestalt of values, beliefs, and specific behaviors that produce the desired capacity.

A huge benefit of modeling capabilities is that they tend to be nonlinear in application. You can model a particular skill and apply it to a variety of different situations, tasks, or contexts.

We can understand how skills are organized using the TOTE model. The TOTE model provides a feedback loop between goals, the choices and means to accomplish those goals, and the evidence used to assess progress towards those goals.

According to the TOTE model, all mental and behavioral programs revolve around having a fixed goal and a variable means to attain that goal. As we think, we set goals in our mind, either consciously or unconsciously, and develop a TEST for when that goal has been achieved.

If the goal hasn't been achieved, then we OPERATE to change something or do something to get closer to the goal.

When our TEST criteria have been satisfied, we then EXIT onto the next step.

In order to model a particular skill or performance, we must identify each of the key elements of the TOTE related to that skill or performance:

- The performer's goals.
- The evidence and evidence procedures used by the performer to determine progress towards that goal.
- The set of choices used by the performer to get to the goal and the specific behaviors used to implement those choices.
- The way the performer responds if the goal is not initially achieved.

When it comes to modeling the TOTE elements of an exceptional performer, there are different levels we can consider such as the ones previously mentioned. We can consider the performer's goals in terms of behavior, capability, beliefs and values, etc. Different levels of goals require different levels of evidence and operations and have different levels of problems.

Some skills and capabilities are made up of other skills and capabilities. In that case, each sub-skill would have to be modeled separately. If you wanted to become a great chess player, you would have to master several skills such as visualization, calculation, evaluating, planning, etc.

We can apply the modeling process to different levels of complexity with respect to different skills and capabilities.

Here are some examples:

Simple behavioral skills: Specific, concrete, observable actions that take place within a short period of time, anywhere from a few seconds to a few minutes. Simple skills include things like getting into a particular state, shooting a basket, brushing your teeth, etc.

Simple cognitive skills: Specific, easily identifiable, and testable mental processes which occur within a short period of time. Examples include remembering names, spelling, and acquiring simple vocabulary.

Simple linguistic skills: recognition and use of key words, phrases, and questions.

Complex behavioral skills: A combination of simple behavioral actions done in a particular way. Examples include performing surgery, making a presentation, acting a part in a film, etc.

Complex linguistic skills: The skilled use of language in a highly dynamic, often spontaneous, situation. Examples include persuasion, negotiation, verbal reframing, storytelling, etc.

Complex Cognitive skills - Those which require a synthesis or sequence of other simple thinking skills. Examples include solving a math problem, designing a house, planning a wedding, etc.

Before doing any sort of modeling, one must consider the level, or chunk size, they will be focusing on. Distinctions and procedures for modeling one level of skill may be ineffective at modeling a different level.

* * *

Modeling Methodology

Phases of the Modeling Process

Before we dive into the specifics of modeling, it may be useful if we got a high-level overview of how modeling works. Modeling can be broken up into 3 distinct phases. There's also some preparation we need to do beforehand to ensure we get started off on the right foot.

Let's go over each one.

Preparation

Select a person who has the capability you wish to model.

You must then determine the following:

- The context in which you will do the modeling.
- Where and when you will have access to the person being modeled.
- What relationship do you want with the person being modeled.
- What state you will be in while doing the modeling.
- Establishing the appropriate conditions, anchors, and lifelines, that will allow you to fully commit to the project.

Phase 1: Unconscious Uptake

In this phase, you are to engage the person being modeled in an example of the desired performance or capability within the appropriate context. You start modeling them by going into "second position" (more on that later) in order to build intuitions about the skills the person is demonstrating.

You're not looking for any specific patterns in this phase. Simply take on the physiology and posture of the model and attempt to identify yourself with him or her internally. Don't try to consciously understand what they're doing. Not yet.

A useful state to adopt in this phase is the state of "not knowing". This is where you drop all previous mental maps and assumptions with reference to one's ongoing experience. Once you have a good set of intuitions from being in "second position" with the person you're modeling, you want to arrange for a context where you can use the skill you've been modeling.

Try out the skill within that context "as if" you're the person you've been modeling. Then, try to achieve the same result by just being "yourself". This will give you a "double description" of the particular skill you're modeling. When the result you get is roughly the same as those the person being modeled gets, then the first phase will be complete.

Phase 2: The Subtraction Process

In this phase, the goal is to sort out what is essential in the model's behavior versus what is unnecessary and be explicit about the strategies and behaviors you modeled. You can use your "first position" (aka first-person) behaviors as a reference since you're able to get similar results to the person being modeled.

Your main task is to clarify and define the specific cognitive and behavioral steps that are required to produce the desired results within the chosen context. You also need to systematically leave out pieces of any of the behaviors or strategies you've identified in order to see what makes a difference. Anything that you leave out that doesn't make any difference to the responses you get is not essential to the model. When you leave out something that does make a difference to the results you get, then you've found a crucial part of the model.

Once you've completed this stage, you will have a "triple description" of the model: you will have a minimum model of how you replicate the model's capabilities for yourself i.e. "first position", you will have "second position" intuitions of the model's capabilities that you developed from placing yourself in his or her shoes, and you will have a "third position" perspective from which you can notice the difference between the way you replicate the model's capabilities and how that person manifested the capability in his or her original way.

Phase 3: Design

In the final phase of modeling, you take everything you've learned from the previous phases and design a context and procedure which enables others to learn the skills you have modeled, and thus be able to get the results that the person who served as the model has been able to achieve. To produce the design, you must integrate all 3 perceptual positions, first, second, and third.

Rather than mimic or imitate the specific steps followed by the person being modeled, it is generally more effective to create the appropriate reference experience for the learners that will help them discover and develop the particular "circuits" they will need to perform the skill effectively.

Different people have different levels of conscious and unconscious competencies as their starting states. Some may be able to combine multiple steps of a procedure together into one step, while others may need a particular step broken down into sub-skills.

Steps of the Modeling Process

Another way to look at modeling is through an 8-step process. The first 6 steps cover both the first and second phases of the modeling process we mentioned previously. The last 2 steps deal primarily with the design phase of the modeling process.

Here they are:

Step 1. Engage the skill to be modeled within the appropriate context.

Step 2. Gather information from multiple perspectives.

Step 3. Filter for relevant features and patterns.

Step 4. Organize the patterns into a coherent structure/model.

Step 5. Test the usefulness and effectiveness of the model by trying them out in specific situations and contexts to make sure you achieve the desired result.

Step 6. Reduce the model to its simplest form that will produce the desired result.

Step 7. Identify the best procedures to transfer, or install, the specific skills identified in the modeling process.

Step 8. Determine the most appropriate instruments to measure the results of the model, and find the limits or edge of the model's validity.

NLP Modeling Perceptual Positions

There are 4 primary positions from which information is gathered:

First Position: "My Perspective" - Trying something out for ourselves and exploring the way we do it.

Second Position: "Your Perspective" - Standing in the shoes of the person to be modeled and attempting to think and act like the other person as much as possible.

Third Position: "Meta Position" - We observe the person being modeled as they interact with other people (ourselves included) as an uninvolved witness. We suspend personal judgments and notice only what our senses perceive.

Fourth Position - "Group Referencing" - Perceiving a situation from the perspective of the whole system, or the "relational field" involved in the situation. It's an intuitive synthesis of all prior perspectives in order to get a sense of the entire gestalt.

At the very least, you need the first three perceptual positions for effective behavioral modeling. Perceiving a situation from multiple perspectives allows one to gain broader insight and understanding with respect to that event or behavior.

Implicit vs. Explicit Modeling

Behaviors can be modeled either implicitly or explicitly.

Implicit modeling involves moving to "second position" with the modeling subject. You're stepping into that person's shoes and adopting their perspective as if it's your own. From here, you can start building personal intuitions about that individual's subject experience. This is a more unconscious form of modeling and is used to examine behavior as a whole.

Implicit modeling tends to be analog in nature and is comparable to a child's perspective. It is an inductive process where we take in and perceive patterns of the world around us.

Explicit modeling involves moving to "third position" to describe the explicit structure of the modeling subject's experience so that it can be transferred to others. This is considered a more conscious form of modeling and one of its main goals is to break down the behavior into its component parts.

We need both explicit and implicit modeling in order to model effectively. Without the implicit phase, there is no effective intuition base from which to build an explicit model. Without the explicit phase, the information that has been modeled cannot be turned into tools and techniques to be transferred to others.

Implicit modeling is more than enough if you want to help a person develop personal, unconscious competence with the desired behavior. If you want to create a technique, procedure, or skill set, that can be taught or transferred to others, then explicit modeling is required.

NLP itself was born from both implicit and explicit modeling. It started off with Richard Bandler implicitly modeling Fritz Perls and Virginia Satir through the use of videotapes and direct experience. Even though he was good at what he did, he couldn't figure out exactly how he was doing it.

John Grinder was responsible for the explicit modeling. As I mentioned at the beginning of this chapter, Grinder made an offer to Bandler that enriched both of them in the process. Bandler showed Grinder what he was doing, and Grinder explained to Bandler what Bandler was doing.

Elicitation

Elicitation is how we gather information and identify relevant features and patterns related to the TOTEs of the person being modeled.

In addition to questionnaires and interviews, it's useful to take a more active role in gathering information like role-plays, simulations, and "real life" observation of the expert in the appropriate context.

The most common NLP elicitation methods either has the person recall and relive a specific experience or carry out a task that presupposes or triggers a particular capability, strategy, resource, or problem. Going back to our chess example, we can ask Magnus to recall a time when he was playing a chess game or we can have him play chess against a computer on the spot.

One advantage of the first method is that it allows the modeling subject to gain some distance from the experience in order to reflect on its structure. If there are aspects of the experience that are unpleasant, it will be easier for them to dissociate.

The disadvantage of the first method is that it may give mixed or contaminated signals because the person has to continually go through the process of recall. They may move in and out of the state being accessed which may create confusion for the viewer.

There's also a lot of filtering (i.e. deleting, distorting, and generalizing) that occurs as they are determining what to access and present to others.

The second method's main advantage is that it provides immediate "higher quality" information about the experiences or states to be explored and utilized. There's less conscious filtering and more spontaneous, unconscious cues available.

The main disadvantage of the second method is that the modeling subject tends to get caught up in the content of the experience and is unable to reflect on the process and develop metacognition. There's also the risk that the modeling subject becomes overly self-conscious about what they're doing, which may lead to discomfort and dissociation from the experience.

Finding Relevant Patterns

A particular skill or capability, regardless of its level of sophistication or complexity, is made up of several dimensions relating to the functions defined by the TOTE. Successful performance of any type requires the ability to conceptualize, analyze, observe, follow procedures, interact with others, and manage relationships, to some degree.

Conceptualization, Analysis, and Observation are necessary for creating effective TESTs. They relate to establishing goals and determining evidence for success. Following procedures, interacting with others, and managing relationships, are aspects of the "Operations" necessary to effectively reach the goal and satisfy the evidence needed for the "TEST" phase of a particular TOTE.

Here's a breakdown of each dimension:

Conceptualization – The ability to conceptualize the whole and relate or fit something into the larger framework.

- What is the purpose of the skill or ability?
- When would you use it? Under what circumstances?
- How does it fit with other competencies?

Analysis – The ability to break something down to its component parts; to categorize its elements.

- What distinctions are most relevant to successfully performing this skill?
- What do those distinctions indicate?

Observation – The ability to gather information in real-time.

- What is most relevant to observe to successfully perform this skill?
- What, specifically, do you need to be able to observe?
- What cues or patterns are most important?

Following procedures – The ability to recall and enact a sequential set of steps that leads to a certain outcome.

- What is the key sequence of actions necessary to successfully

perform this skill? At what level or chunk size are they?
- When and where is it important to follow the sequence of steps precisely? When and where is it important to be flexible?
- To what degree do particular steps rely on particular observations?

Interacting with others - The ability to systematically elicit and react to the ongoing behavioral response of others.

- Which possible reactions (on your part) go with which actions initiated by others? What is the intended result of those reactions?
- What particular actions (on your part) are intended to elicit particular reactions from others? What is the desired result of those reactions?
- What cues let you know when it is time to act, react or change actions?

Managing relationships - The ability to recognize and select appropriate behavior in relation to roles, norms, contexts, etc.

- Under which conditions is it important to vary the pattern of interaction?
- How does the internal state, both within yourself and others, influence and alter what you do or how you do it?
- What desired state, both within yourself and others, is the intended result of the procedure or interaction?

Getting the answers to these questions will help you determine what needs to be taught or provided in order to transfer the capability to others and what will be the evidence that the capability has transferred over.

Finding relevant patterns involve 2 key processes: feature detection and pattern recognition.

Let's cover each one.

Feature Detection

Features are specific qualities or characteristics that we decide to filter for as we're modeling. This includes characteristics like rep systems, linguistic patterns, eye movements, and so on.

The features we look for determine the kind of patterns we find.

Here are the most common features used in the NLP modeling process:

- Physiology - Postural patterns, gestures, eye movements, and nonverbal patterns like voice tone and tempo.
- Cognitive Strategies - Noticing any particular rep systems, sub-modality patterns, and habitual cognitive sequences.
- Meta-Program Patterns - General organizational patterns like time perception, relationship to significant other, orientation towards, goals, etc.
- Meta-Patterns - Patterns in the way that the modeling subject communicates or relates to others involved in the situation.

We can classify distinctions in terms of their level of capability that is the focus of a particular modeling project:

- Simple Behavioral - Specific physical cues and actions.
- Simple Cognitive - Rep systems and modalities.
- Simple Linguistic - Meta Model patterns and predicates
- Complex Behavioral - Perceptual Positions.
- Complex Cognitive - Meta Program Patterns and Logical Levels.
- Complex Linguistic - Sleight of Mouth Patterns

Pattern Recognition

Pattern recognition is the process or procedures used to identify the particular features or distinctions that are the most important for achieving a goal or result.

The most fundamental way to accomplish this is to find a group of people that demonstrate the desired capability or are able to achieve the desired result and find the similarities and differences between them with respect to the features and characteristics you want to explore. Your main goal is to determine the specific features that are common to the processes used by all of the individuals being modeled.

In NLP, there's a method called contrastive analysis, which involves observing which features are always present when a particular result is achieved and which are always absent when a result is not achieved. For example, a person may notice during their creative state that they have constructed visual images and positive internal self-talk. When they are unable to reach that state, there are no such images and the presence of a critical internal voice.

Contrastive analysis is not a foolproof method. For instance, one can use contrastive analysis to show that the main works of genius were done by white Caucasian males of European descent. However, this does not mean that women and non-European people are incapable of producing works of genius.

Defining A Modeling Project

Here's a typical sequence of steps for defining a modeling project:

1. Conduct a needs analysis to determine the specific issues, contexts and skills to be addressed.
2. Select the individuals to be modeled.
3. Set up and carry modeling scenarios and procedures in order to engage the capabilities and performance to be examined and gather the necessary information.
4. Identify the relevant patterns in the behaviors, strategies, beliefs, etc. of the individuals that have been modeled.
5. Organize the patterns that have been discovered into a descriptive and prescriptive structure.
6. Experimentally test and refine the model by trying it out in relevant context(s) to see if it achieves the desired result.
7. Design effective installation/intervention procedures and tools in order to transfer and apply the key elements of the model to others.
8. Measure the results obtained by applying the model.

Throughout your modeling project, it is important to define your evidence and evidence procedure through each phase, including preparation.

Here are some useful questions to ask yourself at each stage:

Preparation

- What criteria will you use (have you used) to identify the individual(s) you will be modeling?
- How do (will) you know that the person(s) to be modeled have the desired skill?
- How do (will) others know that the person(s) to be modeled have the desired skill?

Phases 1 and 2 (Gathering info via implicit and explicit modeling)

- What criteria will you use to know that you have effectively modeled the capability?
- How does the person being modeled know that he or she has the desired skill or has achieved the desired result?
- How do (will) you know that you have learned the skill possessed by the model(s)?
- How will others know that you have learned the skill possessed by the model(s)?

Phase 3 (Design)

- What criteria will you use to know you have effectively transferred the ability?
- How will you know that others have learned the skill possessed by the model?
- How will others know that they have learned the skill possessed by the model?

Answering these questions will help you determine and design the most effective modeling processes.

* * *

Modeling Strategies

Modeling strategies are subprocesses within the overall NLP Modeling methodology. They tend to be used during explicit modeling or when creating tools and procedures to transfer capabilities to others.

Modeling strategies utilize both inductive and deductive processes. Inductive processes involve perceiving the world around us. Deductive processes are those through which we describe and act based on our perceptions. The difference between inductive and deductive processes is the same as the difference between understanding a language versus speaking it.

Micro Modeling Strategies

Micro Modeling Strategies involve modeling pieces of a specific skill such as a simple behavioral, simple cognitive, or a simple linguistic ability.

Here's a simple 3-step process for micro modeling:

1. Identify the skill you want to find out about.
2. Have the person to be modeled demonstrate an example of that skill in a specific context.
3. Elicit the person's TOTE for applying that skill in that context.

TOTE Questions

- What is the context in which you commonly use the skill to be modeled?
- What are the goals and objectives that guide your actions as you apply the skill in this context?
- What do you use as evidence to know that you are accomplishing your goals?
- What do you do to get to those goals? - what are some specific steps and activities that you use to achieve your goals in this context?
- When you experience unexpected problems and difficulties in achieving your goals in this context, what specific steps or activities do you take to correct them?

Macro Modeling Strategies

Macro Modeling Strategies involve identifying component skills of a more complex or involved ability such as a complex behavioral, complex cognitive, or complex linguistic ability.

Here's a 3-step process for Macro Modeling:

1. Engage the person in a context that requires the ability.
2. Identify specific behavioral examples and demonstrations of the ability to be modeled.
3. Starting with the behavior, elicit various levels of the process (how, why, who) that support the behavior.

Multi-level Modeling Questions

- What is the context or environment you are exploring? When and where does the capability or activity occur?
- What are the specific behaviors with the capability that you're exploring? What aspects of the behavior are particularly significant in order to achieve the desired result?
- What internal thoughts and capabilities are associated with that behavior? How do you think when you are acting in that way?
- What values are expressed by your behavior and capabilities?
- What beliefs provide motivation for your thoughts and activity?
- Who are you if you engage in those particular beliefs, values, capabilities, and behaviors? What is your identity?
- What is your mission? Who else are you serving with this activity?

- What is your vision of the larger system in which you are pursuing that mission?

Applied Modeling Strategies

An effective applied modeling strategy is made up of 3 parts:

- Identifying key capabilities possessed by the individuals who are able to achieve a certain outcome or result.
- Specifying particular individuals who may benefit from being able to learn those capabilities and achieve those results.
- Defining which of those capabilities are most needed by individuals who require the skill or desire to achieve the result.

One common approach to applied modeling is to identify a need or problem and then find someone who possesses the capabilities and resources necessary to effectively deal with the need or problem.

Another approach involves identifying the capabilities possessed by individuals who are able to achieve a particular outcome, and then identifying a group of individuals who could benefit the most from those capabilities.

Applied modeling can help with putting the information we gathered from other modeling strategies into practice. We can structure this information gathering using a "Present State-Desired State" format known as the SCORE Model.

The SCORE Model allows us to define the essential features of a particular problem space.

Here's a breakdown letter-by-letter:

S - Define the Symptoms associated with the present or problem state.

C - What are the Causes of those symptoms?

O - What is the desired Outcome that would replace those symptoms?

R - What are the Resources necessary to transform the symptoms and their causes?

E - What are the long-term Effects of achieving the outcome?

Generally speaking, the symptoms and causes are embodied by people who need or desire the capability to be modeled. The outcome, effects, and resources are embodied by the individuals to be modeled.

Here's a basic applied modeling strategy:

- Identify the full SCORE defining the "problem space" to be addressed by the modeling project.
- Elicit the following:
- A multi-level description of the "problem space" of the individual who need the resource being modeled.
- A multi-level description of the capabilities of the individuals who possess the resources necessary to reach the desired state.
- Transfer the relevant levels of resources possessed by the success-

ful individuals to the individuals needing those capabilities.

Applied Modeling Questions

1. Symptom - What are the specific, measurable, or observable symptoms to be addressed by the modeling project?
2. Causes - What are the causes of those symptoms?
3. Outcomes - What is the outcome or desired state to be reached, that the individual(s) to be modeled is able to demonstrate consistently?
4. What resources does the person being modeled have that allow him or her to:
5. Consistently reach the desired outcome.
6. Deal effectively with the symptoms.
7. Address and transform the causes of the symptom.
8. Move in the direction of longer term positive effects

To Be Elicited From Individuals That Need The Resource

1. Are there any contextual or environmental constraints that the individual who needs the capability must contend with?
2. What specific behaviors are they currently engaged in? What are their problem behaviors?
3. What specific cognitive capabilities are they lacking or have that causes them trouble?
4. What beliefs do they have that either limit or disempower them?
5. What values or hierarchy of values, are the individuals who need

the capability, operating from?
6. How do they perceive themselves?
7. Do they have any sense of mission or vision with which to organize their identity?

To Be Elicited From Individuals Who Have The Resource

1. Are there any contextual or environmental opportunities that the person has?
2. What observable behaviors demonstrated by the person being modeled, are different from those that need the capability?
3. What specific mental capabilities or cognitive strategies are employed by the person being modeled?
4. What beliefs do the person being modeled have that allow them to cope more effectively?
5. What values, or hierarchy of values, does the person being modeled operate from?
6. How does the person being modeled perceive themselves?
7. What type of vision and mission does the person being modeled use to organize their activity?

Applied Modeling and the "Back-Propagation" Process

The final stages of Applied Modeling share many similarities with back-propagation in neural network technology.

Neural networks are computer structures based on the way in which the brain functions. They are typically made of a number of interconnected elements that are used to create a type of model of some pattern or phenomenon. The model is formed as a function of "weights" or the strength of connections between the elements in the network. The "inner" model determines the output of the network.

A common strategy used by neural networks is called back-propagation. To give you an example, let's say a neural network is designed to recognize animals. For argument's sake, the image of a penguin is fed into the network.

The image becomes coded as a pattern of reactions in the network based on the current "weightings" of the interconnections. As a product of this pattern, the network outputs a result, let's say a lion. If there's a discrepancy between the expected result and the actual result, the weightings are adjusted accordingly. The image is fed into the network again and the process repeats itself.

After a number of cycles, the output of the network will begin to match the desired result more often. In other words, the computer has created a useful model, one that achieves the desired result given a particular input.

A similar method is used in NLP to refine a model after it has been established. In the case of NLP, the human being would be the "neural network" and the different elements includes things like rep systems, beliefs, values, language patterns, etc. Focusing on one particular distinction is like the process of giving weight to an element in a computer network. Where we place our attention creates an "attractor" that stimulates "self-organizing" behavior in a person.

For instance, noticing a person's facial expressions rather than the types of clothes they're wearing will alter the way you respond to that person.

Here's how to apply the back-propagation approach to applied modeling:

1. Try out the steps, strategies, and distinctions defined by the model, within the appropriate context.
2. Notice the results you achieve and compare them to the desired result.
3. Adjust the steps and distinctions proposed by the model in order to make a "better approximation".
4. Try out the new adjustments to the model, and continue to repeat the process until you (or the person for whom the model is intended) can achieve the required "threshold" of the desired result.

* * *

Code Congruence

Gregory Bateson, a highly influential figure across many fields like social science, anthropology, linguistics, and others, once said that "If you want to think about something, it is best to think about that thing in the same way in which that thing thunk."

Bateson's understanding of code congruency asserts that the most effective and ecological models are those in which the relationships in the model match the relationships between the system of elements of the phenomenon which we are modeling.

An example of code congruency is the path of the planets. When people believed that Earth was the center of the solar system, they had to come up with complicated math equations to account for the movements of the other planets. When things changed and the Sun was placed at the center, the math became a lot simpler and more elegant.

Models which are not code congruent may be useful in some cases, but they have their limits.

Code Congruence in Behavioral Modeling

In the early days of NLP, Richard Bandler and John Grinder decided to conduct a Modeling Seminar where they would model the work of Virginia Satir.

They decided to break it up over 2 days. For the first day, Virginia would work with a family in the morning, demonstrating her approach to Family Therapy. Bandler and Grinder would reflect on her work and describe some of the key behavioral and linguistic patterns she had applied during the session. The next morning, she would work with another family, leaving the last afternoon for a final reflection and closing remarks.

The first morning went as expected. Later that afternoon, Bandler and Grinder described how Virginia "anchored" various family members using nonverbal cues, how she led various individuals into certain states, how she created and triggered various responses in the family members, and so on.

The next morning was a complete disaster. Virginia was unhappy with her work and so were the family members and everyone else involved. According to Bateson's code congruence, Bandler and Grinder described Satir's actions in mechanical, cause and effect terms, which is probably not the way that Virginia herself thought about what she did, consciously or unconsciously. Her poor performance on the second day was not brought on by the fact that she was conscious of the process, but rather, because the code used to model her process was not congruent with the structure of the actual process.

Code congruency does not have to do with the accuracy of the content of the code or model. The important thing is that the relationships between the elements and events in the model is congruent with the relationships between the elements and events making up the system we're modeling.

Chapter 6: The Key Language Models

Meta Model

History of the Meta Model

Back in the 1970s, Richard Bandler, one of the co-founders of NLP, and Frank Pucelik learned Gestalt therapy from modeling the founder himself, Fritz Perls. They began teaching it to other students at the University of California but lacked the knowledge of the specific patterns being used.

John Grinder, the other co-founder of NLP, helped dissect the specific patterns they were using by first modeling each of them, to get an unconscious representation of the patterns, and then codified it. They continued their modeling work with Virginia Satir, a world-renowned Family therapist, and noted an overlap with Fritz Perls work.

In 1975, The Structure of Magic was published and the Meta Model was introduced for the first time. It was originally intended to be used by therapists, but it can be applied in a wide range of applications including business, personal development, and coaching/consulting.

The Goal of The Meta Model

The Meta Model is simply that, just a model. But for our purposes, we will be using the Meta Model to help others point their consciousness in more useful directions. We do that by treating their "mental map" (or statement) as a whole map and asking questions that challenge the main idea behind an utterance or statement.

First, there is the sensory-based map which forms an internal representation of everything we see, hear, feel, taste, etc. from a moment-to-moment basis. Secondly, there is the linguistic map which is a symbolic interpretation of the sensory-based map.

In the Structure of Magic, Bandler and Grinder outline what they call the "Universal Model Process", which describes how we form our linguistic maps.

There are 3 distinct elements:

- Deletion – A process which removes portions of the sensory-based mental map and does not appear in the verbal expression.
- Distortion – The process of representing parts of the model differently than how they were originally represented in the sensory-based map.
- Generalization – The way a specific experience is mapped to represent the entire category of which it is a part of.

Chapter 6: The Key Language Models

In the Structure of Magic, Bandler and Grinder make a distinction between "surface structure" and "deep structure", two terms that they borrowed from transformational grammar.

The surface structure refers to the words or utterances that correspond to the internal representation. This is where we notice the deletions, distortions, and generalizations that gives us insight into their model of the world. The deep structure is the pure experience which the surface structure is based upon. It exists at an unconscious level.

Traditionally, therapists used the Meta Model to help their clients recover the deep structure in their language or "restore the well-formedness conditions of the surface structure."

By using the Meta Model challenge questions, we're able to help someone connect to the deep structure where more resources are present.

Transformational Grammar has been largely abandoned due to numerous flaws but we'll cover those in more detail in the following section titled "The Meta Model Revisited".

The Meta Model Compass

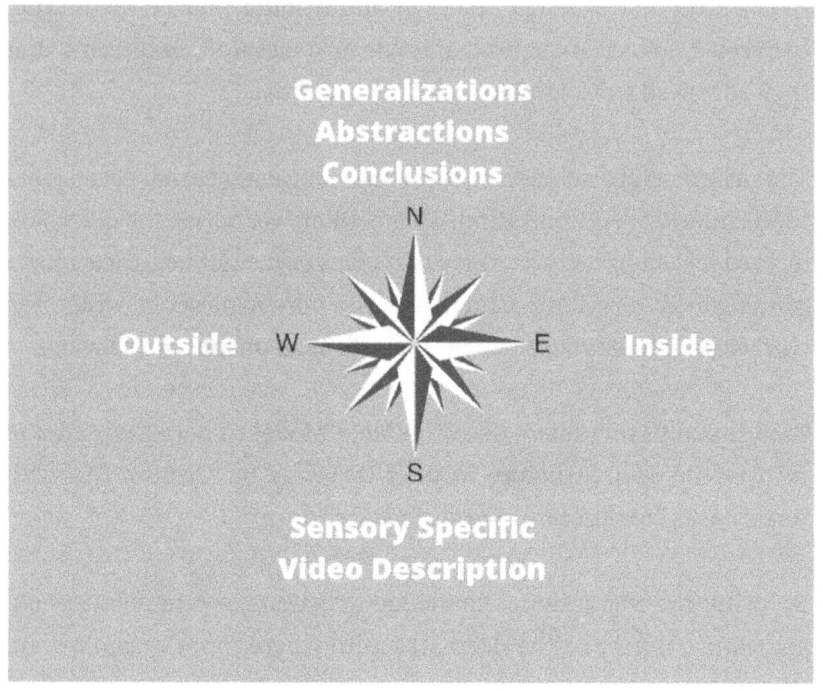

I want you to start thinking of the Meta Model in terms of a compass. This concept was originally formulated by NLP Master Trainer Michael Breen.

On the north end of the compass, we have generalizations, conclusions, abstractions, and summaries. This is a high-level overview of someone's thought.

On the southern end of the compass, we have the sensory-specific information. This is the kind of information that could be picked up on a video camera, other than taste and smell. In other words, just the facts.

Every statement that someone makes is relatively specific or relatively abstract in relation to the context that they are speaking about. By the time you hear what someone has said, billions of processes have already taken place in their brains. What you hear is a conclusion based on many neurological processes.

On the eastern end of the compass, we have what's called "inside the map."

"Inside of the map" is the type of information that a journalist would look for: who, what, when, where, and how. We can usually infer this information from what someone has said.

On the west side, we have the patterns that relate to what's outside of someone's map or model. These are the linguistic elements from inside the map or model that someone cannot perceive.

We will be using this compass as we go through each pattern to demonstrate how each pattern relates to the compass.

As an added note, there are also patterns that fall on the "backbone" of the compass which is neither inside nor outside of the map or model.

Presuppositions

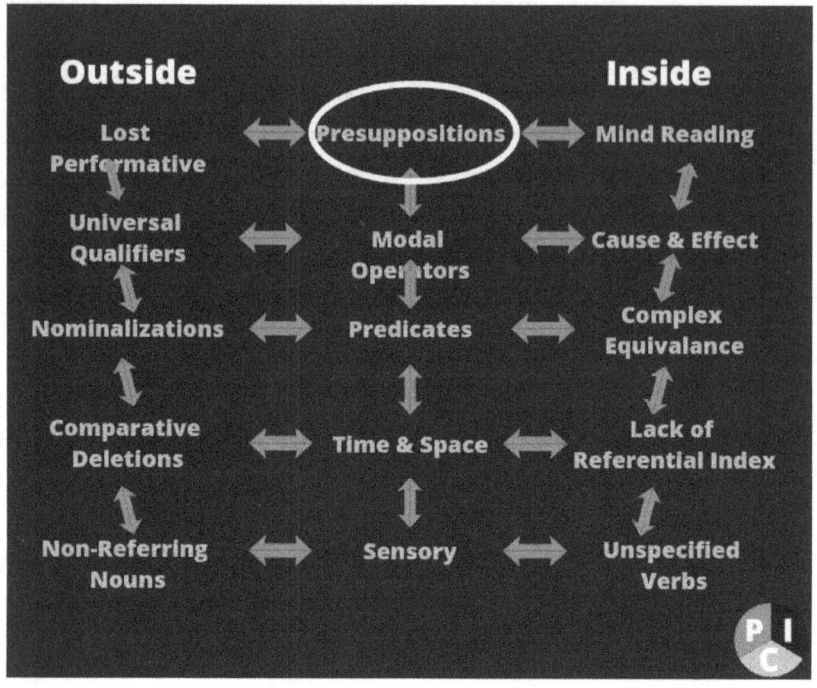

Every statement that is made is a claim to knowledge. All of the language patterns in the Meta Model act as presuppositions in the statement that is made.

As a quick exercise, I'm going to give you a sentence and I want you to presuppose what has to be there in order for the statement to make sense.

Here it is:

"The cat sat on the mat."

Think about it for a sec. For starters, we have to presuppose there's an entity called a "cat". We have to presuppose there's an object or entity called "mat". Lastly, we have to presuppose there's a relationship between the two entities called "sat".

Because presuppositions exist within every single utterance, we're going to place it at the top of the Meta Model.

In the Structure of Magic, Bandler and Grinder outlined 29 syntactic environments, which are places within an utterance or sentence, where presuppositions can live. The problem with this approach is that it makes learning the Meta Model seem a lot more complicated than it really is.

For our purposes, we won't be going over each one, but focus on the general idea of presuppositions.

Mind Reading

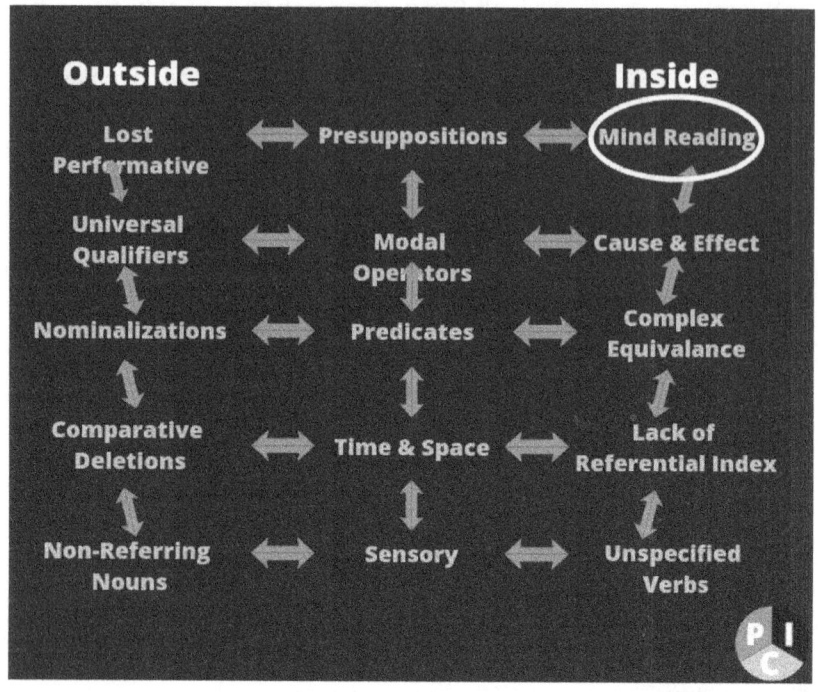

This is the first pattern that we look at from inside of the map or model.

A Mind Read is a claim that's made without stating how you know. In order to challenge this language pattern, we must first assume that in order for someone to make a particular claim, they have to have a way of making that claim. Also, if someone is making a claim about something that is less than useful, isn't helpful, or it's getting in the way, we can ask someone for the foundation of that claim and make a change in how someone thinks.

Here's how you would challenge a mind read: how do you know?

Asking them how they know allows us to see where they're drawing that information from.

Lost Performative

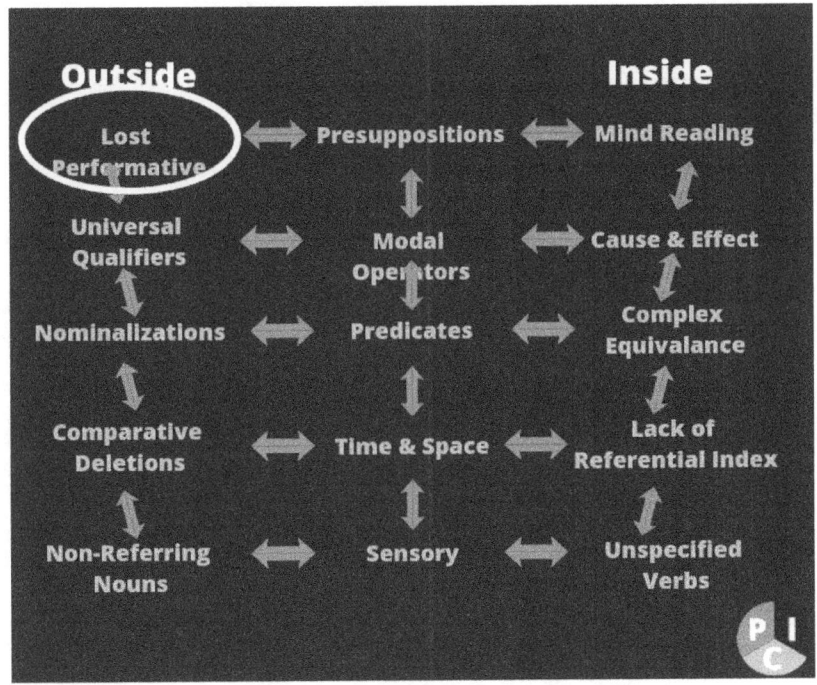

The Lost Performative is the first pattern we look at from outside of the map or model. It has the same overarching influence as the Mind Read but from the outside. Challenging this pattern allows you to take a statement from a free-floating reality back to a statement about a specific time, a specific place, and a specific reason.

More often than not, we tend to drop who said it, when they said it, and under what conditions. When we fail to define the scope of a particular statement, our nervous system treats it as a universal, meaning all situations, and at all times.

Here are a few questions for challenging a Lost Performative:

- Who says?
- According to whom?
- Where did you get that from?

Modal Operators

CHAPTER 6: THE KEY LANGUAGE MODELS

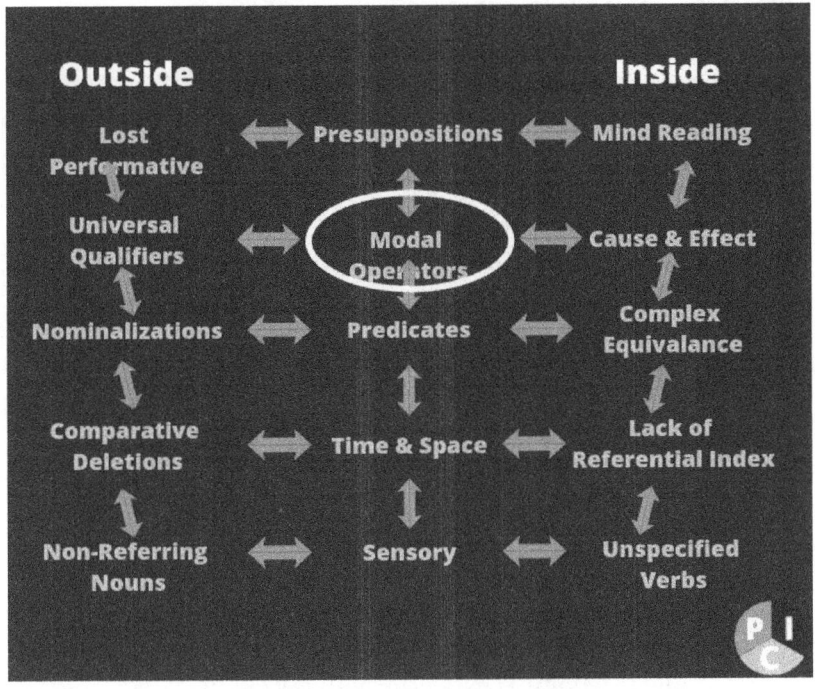

Modal operators describe the mode of operating in a sentence. They show us the boundary of the map or model. You can also learn what motivates someone by the modal operators they use.

There are 3 types we concern ourselves with:

- Possibility – can, could, may, might
- Necessity – should, ought to, must, need to
- Desirability – love, like to

There are a number of ways you can challenge modal operators. First, there's the conventional approach.

For example, someone says, "I can't do something."

You can respond, "What would happen if you could?"

This kind of question provides us information from outside of the map.

You can also respond with, "What stops you?"

This provides us with information from inside of the map.

Here are some other challenge questions you can ask:

- How do you know that you can't? (Mind Reading)
- According to whom? (Lost Performative)

By the way, when someone says that they can't do something, they're literally saying "I can engage in the act of not doing x." Something to keep in mind.

Universal Qualifiers

CHAPTER 6: THE KEY LANGUAGE MODELS

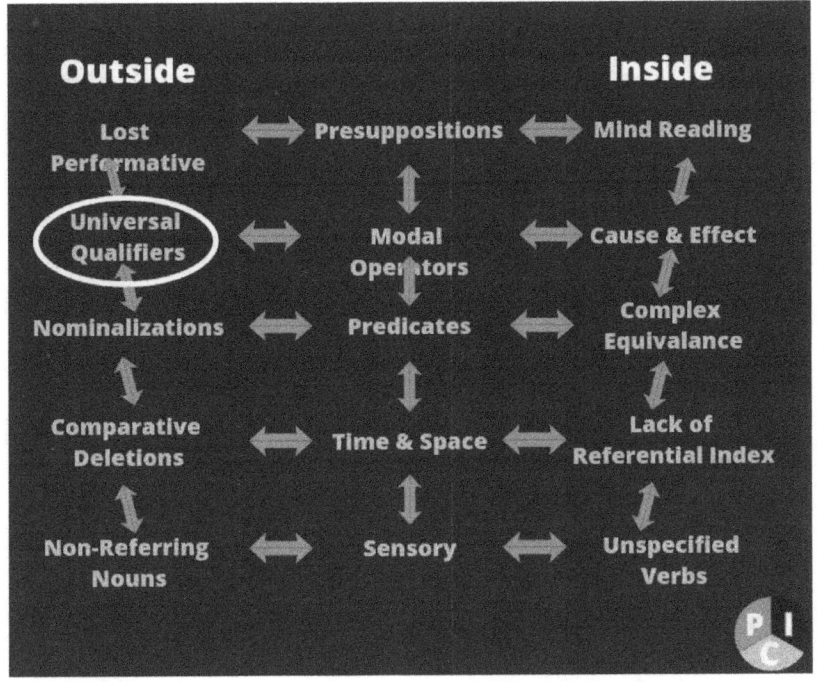

Universal Qualifiers define the scope of the map. Some examples include "every", "all", and "only". There are also times when universal qualifiers aren't being used explicitly. Unless someone offers a form of qualification, there is an implied or inferred universality to what they're saying.

In order for a statement with a universal qualifier to be valid, there cannot exist a single counterexample.

To challenge a universal qualifier (implied or explicit), come up with a counterexample that could be true, based on what they say.

Cause & Effect

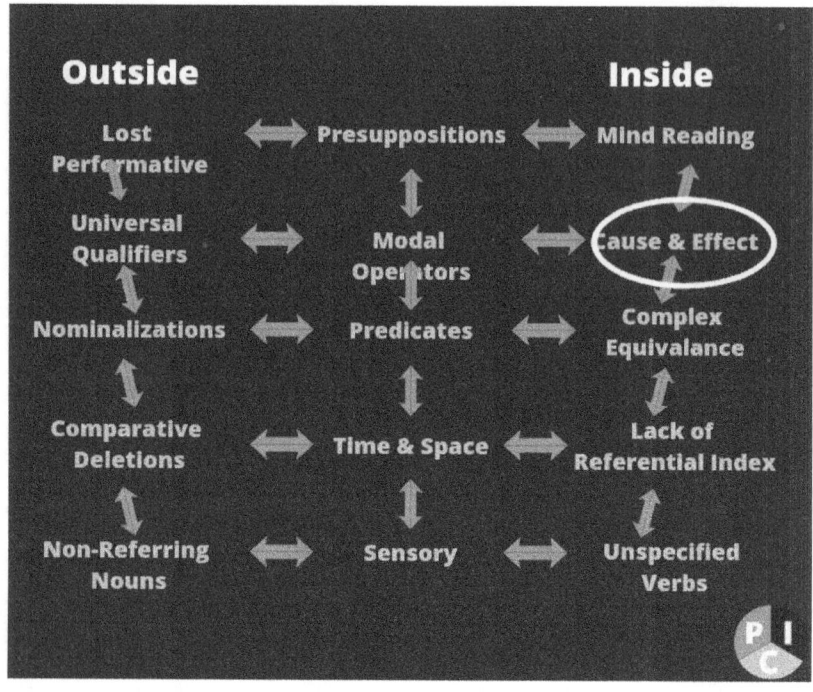

Cause & Effect gives us the structure for how the model works. The basic structure for cause and effect is "if x, then y". On the "x" side, we have the sum total of evidence that points to "y" as the outcome. It could be one thing, or it could be several things, depending upon the belief.

For more information on challenging the cause and/or effect, check out the Sleight of Mouth language patterns which we'll cover in a later section.

Nominalization

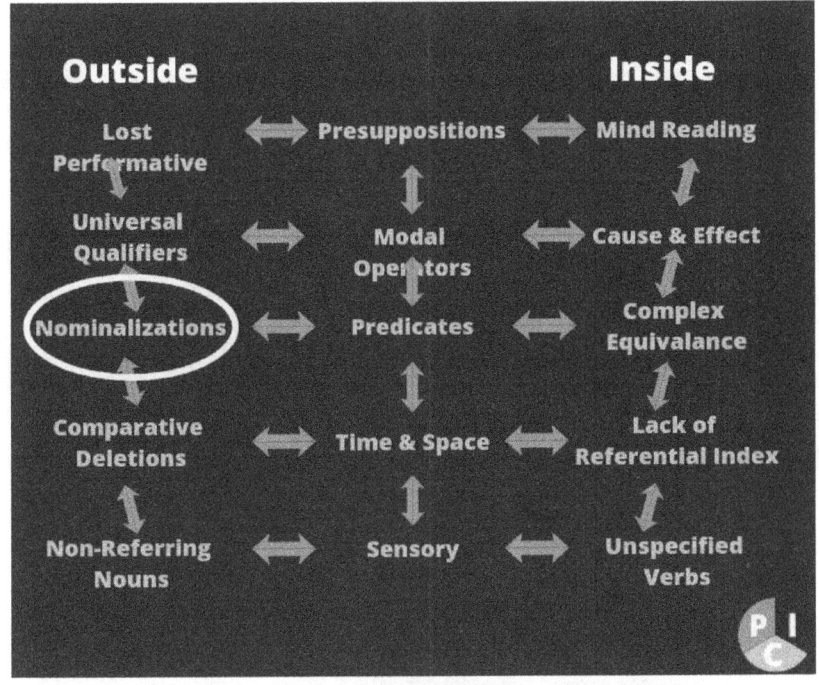

Nominalization allows us to take complex activities and put it together into one thing so we can think about it. If you're unsure if a word is a nominalization, use the wheelbarrow test. Any noun that you can't put into a wheelbarrow is a nominalization.

Here are some examples of nominalizations:

education – educate
   conclusion – conclude
   demonstration – demonstrate

If a nominalization is being problematic, it can prevent someone from taking effective action. To solve this, put the nominalization back into verb form.

Predicates

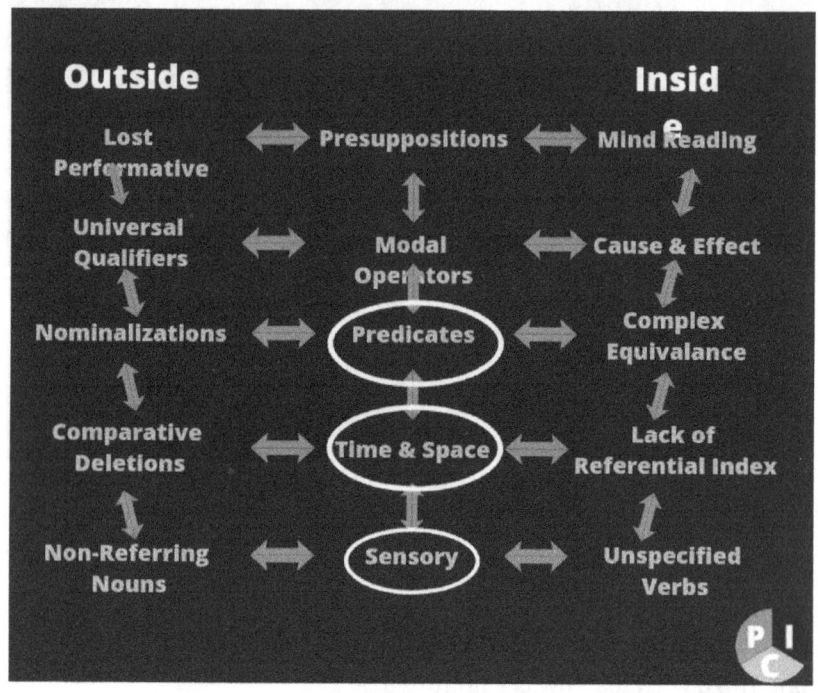

Predicates are words that tell something about the subject.

We can use these words to influence what kind of representations someone makes in their mind.

There are 2 main types of predicates: Time/Space and Sensory.

CHAPTER 6: THE KEY LANGUAGE MODELS

Time/Space predicates allow you to place things in regards to submodalities.

Here are a few examples of each:

- Time – before, look back, happened
- Space – here, there, inside

Sensory predicates are words that imply sensory information.

In NLP, there are 5 major representation systems: Visual, Auditory, Kinesthetic, Olfactory and Gustatory.

Each type of sensory predicate corresponds to one of the representation systems.

Here are a few examples of sensory predicates:

- Visual – review, out of sight, show me, colorful
- Auditory – Outspoken, say, Shout, unheard of
- Kinesthetic – Heartwarming, Firmly, Solid, Gripping
- Olfactory & Gustatory – stinking, fragrant, sweet, stale

Complex Equivalence

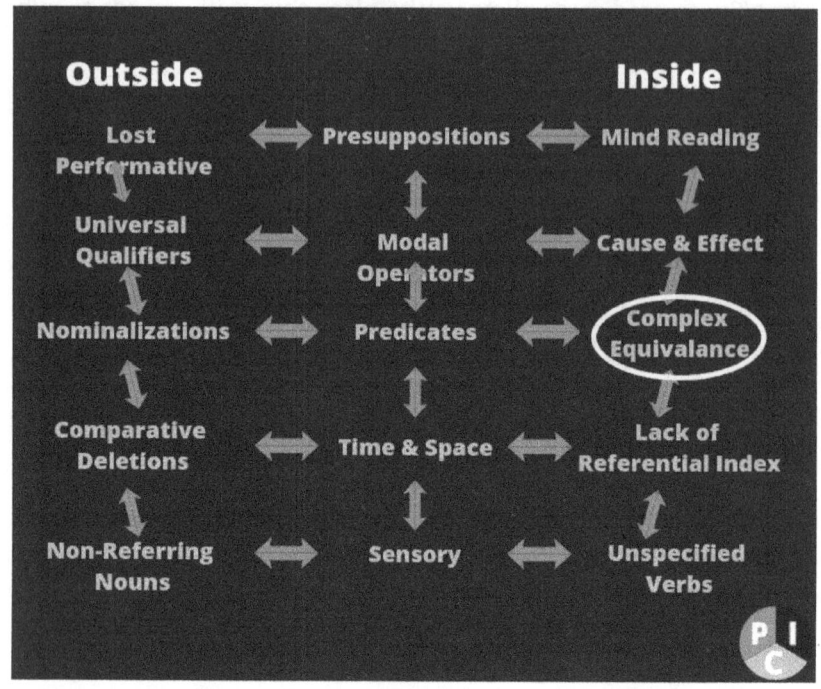

A complex equivalence occurs when a person equates a particular, qualitative word and their experience of the world around them.

Here's an example: "I just missed my appointment. I'm such a disappointment".

In this example, "missing the appointment" is the same thing as "being a disappointment".

To challenge a complex equivalence, you simply ask them how they equate the qualitative or descriptive word with their experience of the world around them.

Usually, they will give you a list of things that let them know how those two things are equal. In that list, there will be some sensory-specific language, but you want to look out for nominalizations. This is partly because Nominalizations and Complex Equivalences are on the same level of the Meta Model Compass. Nominalizations describes the bits and Complex Equivalences show how they all fit to mean one thing.

In addition, the Sleight of Mouth language patterns are also great for challenging complex equivalences.

Comparative Deletions

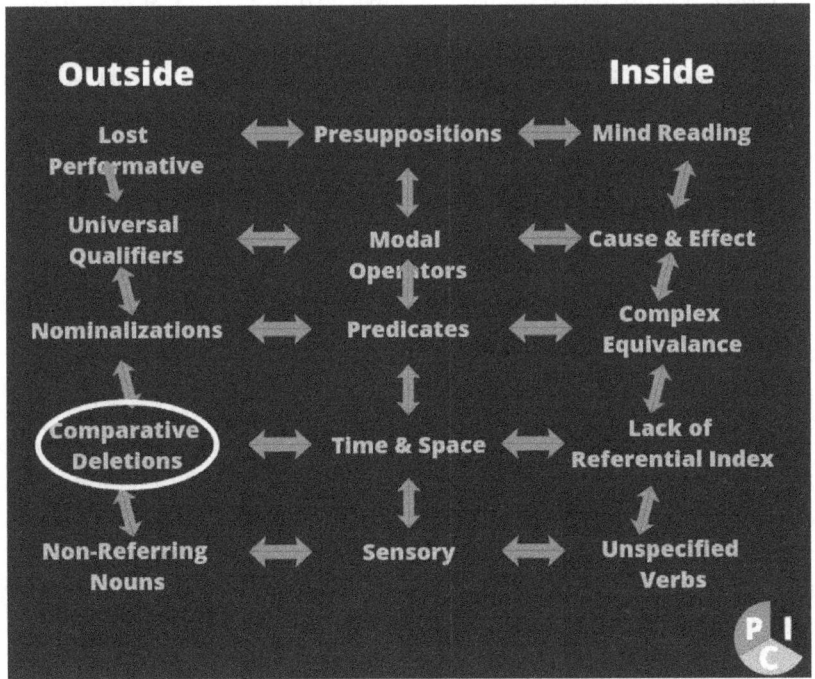

Every evaluation that's made, from the biggest abstractions to the sensory-specific, comes from making comparisons to other things.

Traditionally, this pattern was used for statements that contained phrases like "better than", "worse than", best, etc. However, you can still use this pattern even if there's no explicit mention of a comparison. If there's no standard of comparison mentioned in the map, you can simply ask about it.

Here's an example:

Person A: This is the worst sandwich I ever tasted.

Person B: Compared to what? A sandwich from a five-star restaurant?

By asking for a standard of comparison, you're able to sort out the relative difficulty for that person.

Lack of Referential Index

CHAPTER 6: THE KEY LANGUAGE MODELS

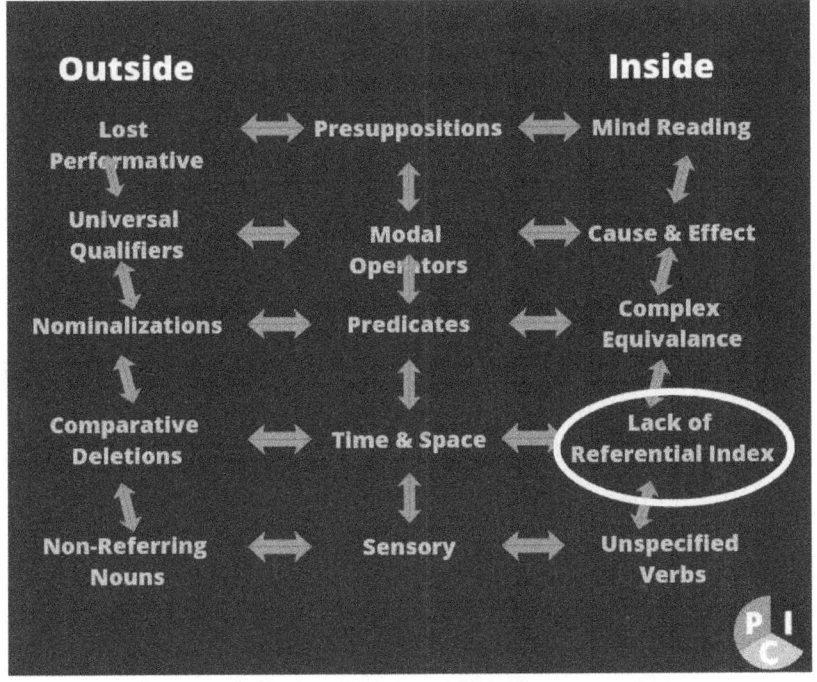

A referential index refers to the subject of the sentence.

Lack of referential index is a language pattern where the "who" or "what" the speaker is referring to isn't specified.

Examples include he, she, it, and they.

To challenge a lack of referential index, ask "who?" or "what, specifically?" to gain clarity on what the speaker is referring to.

Non-Referring Nouns & Unspecified Verbs

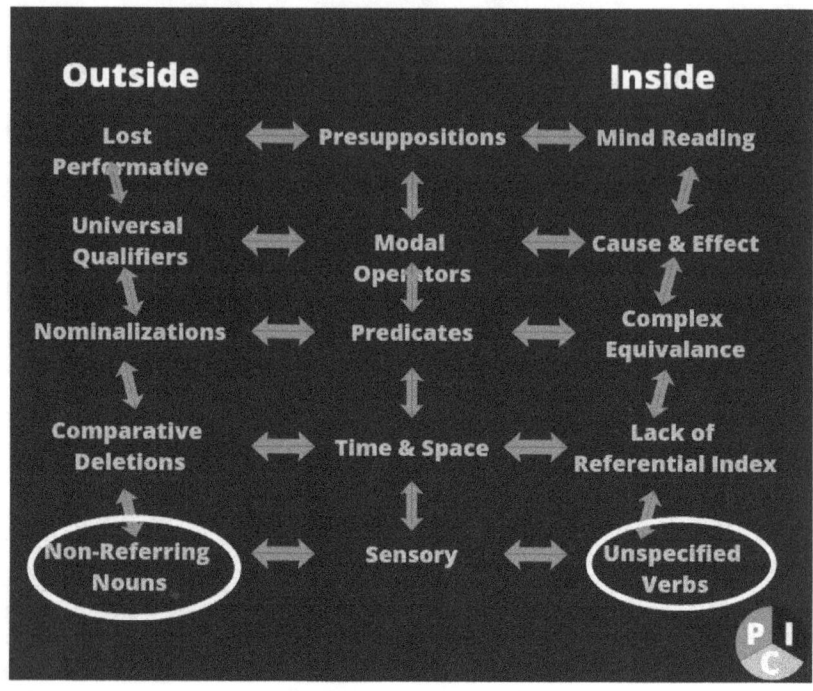

We will present the last two patterns together because they are interrelated with one another. Both of them live at the bottom of the Meta Model, in relation to the compass.

The subject-verb relationship is fundamental to the acts of cognition. We have an inherent need to know what something is and what it's doing.

It's also the first linguistic structure that children learn to generate.

Non-referring nouns are also called Unspecified Nouns.

When we challenge this language pattern, we're able to find out more information about who or what is being talked about.

To challenge a non-referring noun, we use the same questions as those in lack of referential index. The words are the same, but the function is different.

In the case of unspecified verbs, it's important to note that every verb is relatively unspecified. To challenge an unspecified verb, simply ask "How, specifically?" to get more information.

Keep in mind that just because you collect more information about a verb, doesn't provide more understanding about what's going on.

Here's an example: Let's say you're with a guy and he tells you, "My friend hit me."

You ask, "How?"

He responds, "She hit me hard."

You ask, "With what?"

He responds, "With an idea."

You ask, "why?"

He responds, "Because she was trying to help me."

It's not until we ask our third question that we finally realize that the guy is speaking figuratively. This is why it's important to start at the top of the model and then work your way down. Otherwise, you'll end up collecting a bunch of useless information.

* * *

The Meta Model Revisited

Back in April 2019, I wrote a blog post on the Meta Model. In fact, the previous section you just read was based on that blog post. Although much of the information is still valid, I had made an error in regards to the linguistic theory behind the Meta Model. Back when I wrote the post, there was a lot of misinformation and many people were throwing around the same outdated ideas. I pulled what I thought was the best of these ideas together and wrote what I believed was a detailed explanation behind the Meta Model.

My understanding of the Meta Model was vastly expanded thanks to a certain gentleman named Eric Robbie. Eric Robbie has been hailed as the "father of British NLP" and has written much on the subject of NLP. It was thanks to him and his research that I was able to gain a deeper understanding of what the Meta Model is about and the ordering principle behind it.

His work on the Ordering Principle of the Meta Model will be cited throughout this section as a debt of gratitude.

All diagrams that appear in this chapter are credited to Eric Robbie unless otherwise stated.

CHAPTER 6: THE KEY LANGUAGE MODELS

More History of the Meta Model

The Meta Model made its original appearance in The Structure of Magic Vol. 1, written by Richard Bandler and John Grinder, the original co-founders of NLP. 5 years after it was published, Steve Lankton created the first attempted ordering of the Meta Model. It was featured in the appendix of his book Practical Magic.

Lankton's ordering (1980)

Presupposition
Causal Modelling
Mind Reading

operate on

Universal Quantifiers
Generalizations
Lost Performatives
Modal Operators

operate on

Deletions
Referential Index Deletion
Unspecified Verbs
Nominalizations

CHAPTER 6: THE KEY LANGUAGE MODELS

Before Lankton, Robert Dilts created an indirect ordering of the Meta Model. In his rendition, he sorted the Meta Model into 3 common-functional groups:

Dilts's grouping (1978)

Information gathering:
Deletion/ Simple Deletion
Lack of Referential Index
Comparatives Deletion
Unspecified Verb
Nominalization

Limitations of an Individual's Model:
Presuppositions
Modal Operators
Universal Quantifiers
Complex Equivalence

Semantic Ill-Formedness:
Cause–Effect
Mind Reading
Lost Performative

Eric Robbie created his first ordering of the Meta Model based off the works of Lanktons', Dilts', and Cameron-Bandler's ordering (which appeared in the appendix of Happily Ever After, 1978):

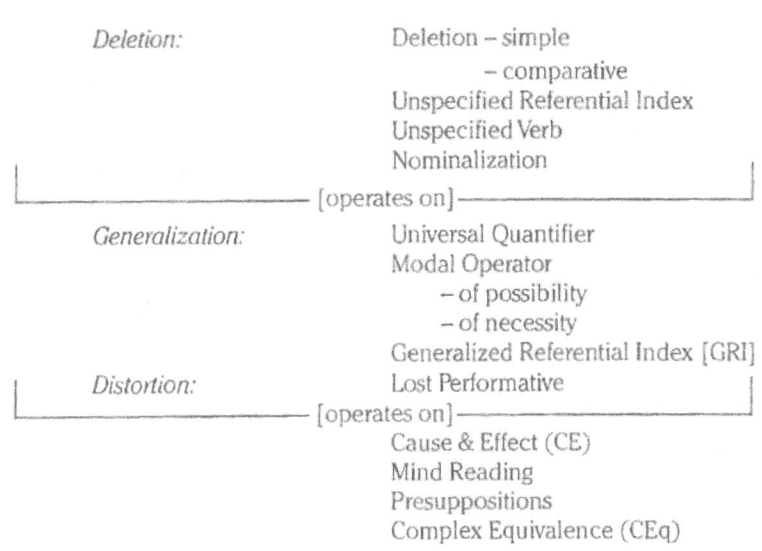

Eric Robbie's ordering ended up catching on and was passed down to several generations of NLP Practitioners. By 1986, it was widely circulated throughout Europe but hadn't made its way to the United States. About 2 years later, Eric had slightly modified his original ordering by moving the Lost Performative to the other side of the "operates on" line. He also began to see presuppositions as a separate class of operator and moved it south to show that it operated on the model as a whole.

In a conversation between Greg Gibson, who was writing the review for the Structure of Magic I, and Richard Bandler, Richard stated that the Meta Model is presented in the inverse order of how one should use it.

Shortly afterward, NLP Trainer Tad James turned his list upside down so that items such as Cause and Effect (CE) and Complex Equivalence (CEq) were at the top of the page, and deletions items were at the bottom. However, he did not offer any rationale for this ordering.

The official ordering of the Meta Model came out in 1987 by Eric Robbie. It was during this time that he presented his ordering for the first time in the United States. Since then, it has become the standard in the field of NLP.

CHAPTER 6: THE KEY LANGUAGE MODELS

DELETION

'Simple' Deletion
Comparative Deletion
Lack of Referential Index
Unspecified Verb
Nominalization

──── [all operate on] ────

GENERALIZATION

Universal Quantifier
Modal Operator of Possibility
Modal Operator of Necessity
Generalized Ref. Index

──── [all operate on] ────

DISTORTION

Lost Performative
Mind Reading
Complex Equivalence
Cause and Effect

──── [operate on] ────

PRE-SUPPOSITIONS

Robbie 1987

X-Bar Theory Crash Course

In the previous section, we mentioned how John Grinder and Richard Bandler make a distinction between deep structure and surface structure. These 2 terms originate from Transformational Grammar, which was initially formulated by Noam Chomsky back in 1965.

Transformational Grammar is a system of language analysis that recognizes the relations among various elements of a sentence and among the possible sentences of a language and uses processes or rules (some of which are called transformations) to express these relationships. (Source: Brittanica)

Surface structure is the sentence in the form that it is heard or written.

Deep structure is an abstract representation that identifies ways that a sentence can be analyzed and interpreted.

Here's a quick example to see how that looks:

Surface Structure: I know a man who flies planes.

Deep Structure: I know a man. The man flies airplanes.

It didn't take long for problems to emerge with this theory. And they were already well-known when the Structure of Magic Vol. 1 came out. Here's the most obvious problem, linguistically speaking: How do you make the nominalized version of a phrase or sentence without breaking all of the "Deep Structure" rules?

To illustrate this, here's an example taken from Horrock's "Bounding Theory and Greek Syntax":

Sentence 1: Bresnan criticized Chomsky

Sentence 2: Bresnan's criticism of Chomsky.

We can see that both of these sentences have the same deep structure. Unfortunately, it is nearly impossible to write out rules that track each step from one sentence to the other.

Here's a few questions that need to be answered:

- How do you get from Bresnan to Bresnan's, with an apostrophe?
- How do you get from criticized, the verb, to criticism, the noun, singular, when it's possible that Bresnan could've had 2 or more criticisms of Chomsky?
- Let's say you manage to go from "criticized" to "criticism". You still have to put an "of" in front of it. Where does that "of" come from? You can't just make it up or pull it out of the sky.

To make matters worse, there are at least 6 or more ways to make a nominalization out of a verb in the English language.

Which is the right one for any given verb?

- Do we add an "-ance" as in "performance"?
- Do we add an "-ment" as in "bewilderment"?

- Do we add an "ism" as in "criticism"?

Then there's the preposition.

If you have to add one, how do you know which one to use?

- Do you add a "to" as in "marriage to"?
- Do you add a "for", as in "proposal for"?
- Do you add an "of" as in "criticism of"?

Even Chomsky later admitted that it's hard to draw a general rule when there is no regular pattern for forming the nominalized word.

In short, there are 2 major problems with the Standard Theory:

1. There were many instances that didn't follow transformational rules.
2. There were instances where Deep Structure couldn't completely give rise to the meaning of the sentence, the way it should.

So, what's the solution?

Instead of thinking of the individual words in sentences, it made more sense to group the words into phrases. Those phrases acted as "language modules" which could be plugged in and out of sentences. This helped to pave the way for various solutions.

CHAPTER 6: THE KEY LANGUAGE MODELS

In Steven Pinker's book "The Language Instinct", he talks about this at length. Modern linguistics has shown there to be a common anatomy in all the world's languages.

First, there's the noun phrase, or NP for short. It's named after the noun that appears in the phrase. As you would expect, the NP owes most of its properties to that one noun.

Here's an example of a noun phrase (credits to Steven Pinker): The cat in the hat

In this example, "the cat in the hat" refers to a kind of a cat, not a kind of hat. The cat is the core meaning of the whole phrase. This special noun is also referred to as the "head" of the phrase.

Verb Phrases, or VP for short, follow a similar pattern.

Here's an example (credits to Steven Pinker): Flying to Canada before the police catch them.

In this phrase, we are talking about the "flying" as opposed to the "catching".

This leads us to the first principle which is that the entire phrase is about what its "head" word is about. The second principle states that sets of players interact with each other in particular ways, each with a specific role.

Here's an example sentence to illustrate this:

Sergey gave the documents to the spy.

In this example, we are not talking about any act of giving. There are 3 entities to account for: Sergey (the giver), the documents (the gift), and a spy (the receiver).

Role-players are formally referred to as arguments, in a logical sense.

Noun phrases can assign roles to one or more role-players. The head and the role-players are joined together in a sub-phrase, which is smaller than a NP or VP. The standard terminology is called N-bar or V-bar, named after the way they are written.

Here's an example of an N-bar:

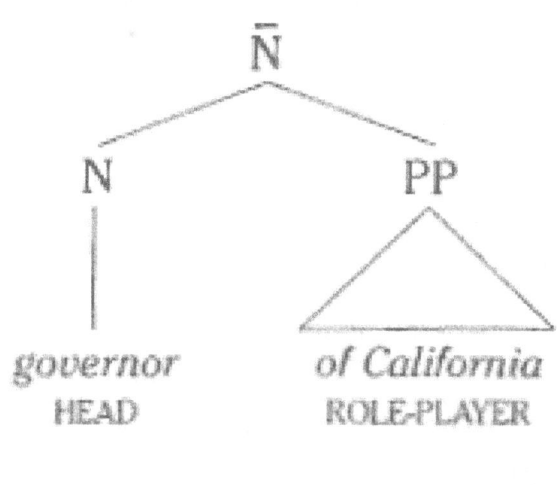

(Diagram Robbie, after Pinker)[2]

Note: the PP stands for Preposition Phrase.

The third ingredient of a phrase is one or more modifiers. Take the phrase "man from New York" as opposed to "governor of Texas". In the latter phrase, to be a governor, you have to govern something. This is where the "California" part comes into play. "From New York" is just an extra piece of information to help identify which man we're talking about.

The distinction between role-players and modifiers dictates how the phrase-structure tree looks. To elaborate, the role-player stays next to the head noun inside of the n-bar, but the modifier goes in a separate branch but stays within the NP "house".

Here's what that looks like:

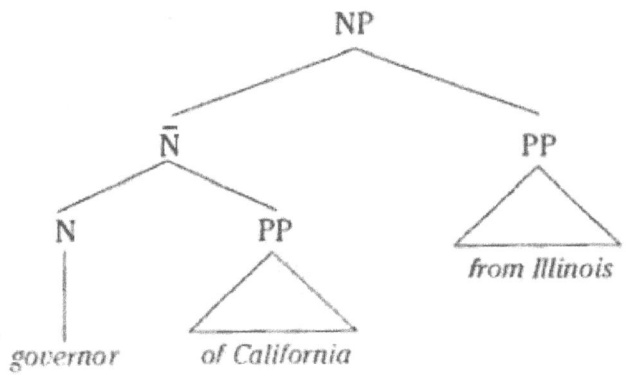

What's true for n-bars and noun phrases is also true for v-bars and verb phrases.

Here's an example (credits to Steven Pinker):

Sergey gave those documents to the spy in the hotel.

"To the spy" is one of the role-players of the verb give. After all, there's no such thing as giving without a getter. "To the spy" lives with the head verb inside of the v-bar. "In a hotel" is a modifier that is kept outside of the v-bar, but is still in the VP. We can say "gave the documents to the spy in a hotel" but not "gave in a hotel the documents to the spy."

The fourth component of a phrase is called the subject, or as linguists call them, SPEC. The word SPEC is short for specifier. The subject is a type of role-player that usually acts as a causal agent (if one exists).

Here's an example (credits to Steven Pinker):

"The guitarists destroy the hotel room"

CHAPTER 6: THE KEY LANGUAGE MODELS

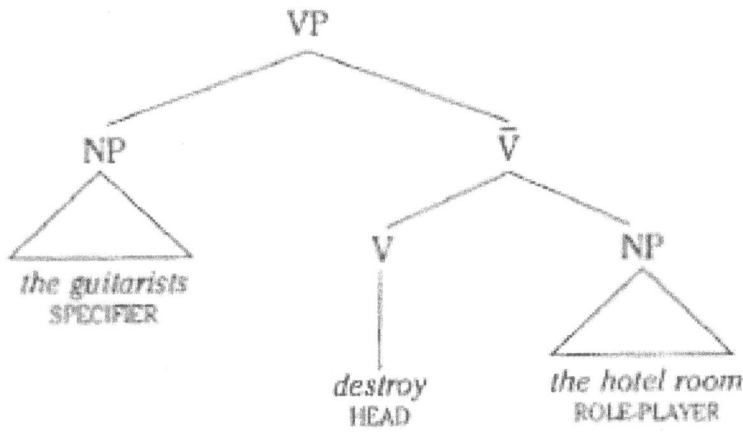

"The guitarists" is the subject or the causal agent where the hotel room is destroyed.

Noun phrases can also have subjects. For example, "The guitarists' destruction of the hotel room".

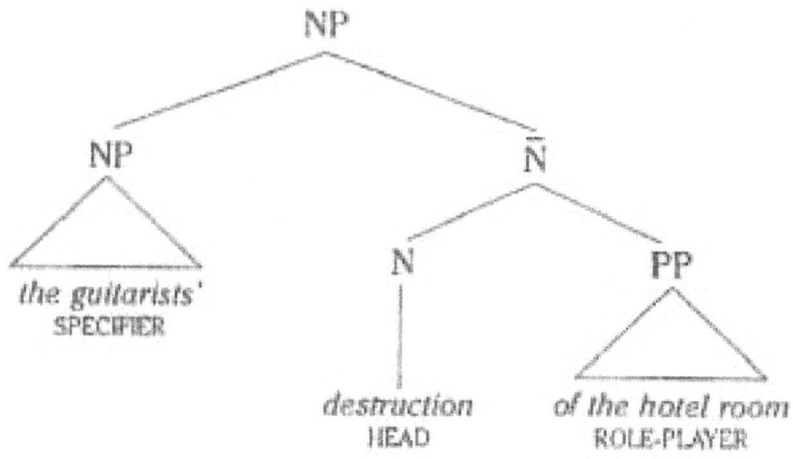

When we use this structure, the nominalization problem is solved because there's no need for a transformation. Also, "tracking each step" is covered by a common anatomy. In other words, there's no change whatsoever. In addition, the choice of ending (e.g. -ance) or linking the appropriate word (e.g. by) has been relocated to the lexicon.

As a quick re-cap, here are the similarities between noun phrases and verb phrases:

- A "head word", which gives the phrase its name and determines what it's about.
- Some role-players, which are grouped with the head inside a head phrase.
- Modifiers, which appear outside of the N-bar or V-bar.
- A subject, also known as a SPEC.
- The same ordering i.e. the noun (or verb) comes before its role-

players.

The same rules apply for Prepositional Phrases (PP) and Adjectival Phrases (AP). An example of a PP would be "in the hotel" where "in" is the head word. An example of an AP would be "afraid of the wolf" where "afraid" is the head word.

The foundations of X-bar theory was laid by Chomsky back in 1970 and was added to by others over the next couple of years. The bulk of the theory was already in existence by the time The Structure of Magic Vol. 1 came out.

The Meta Model Decoded

It's time to get into the good stuff. Let's talk about how the Meta Model relates to the X-bar theory we just described above. To do that, we'll be breaking down the Meta Model into 4 discrete sections and talk about them one by one.

Deletion Patterns

As a quick note, the first group of Meta Model patterns do not all use the same mechanisms. Deletion can happen in one of two places: somewhere in the journey from having a complete experience to forming a complete sentence, or somewhere in the journey from forming a complete sentence to offering spoken words.

Here's a diagram, courtesy of Eric Robbie, which helps illustrate this:

	complete experience	complete 'inner sentence'	what people actually say
Simple Deletion	|<·········>	|<·········>	BIT MISSING
Comparative Deletion	|<·········>	|<·········>	BIT MISSING
Lack of Ref. Index	NOT TELLING |<·········>	|<·········>	
Incompletely Specified Verb	POOR TELLING |<·········>	|<·········>	
Nominalization	NOT TELLING |<·········> POOR TELLING	|<·········>	& MOST BITS MISSING AS WELL

It should also be noted that the Structure of Magic Vol. 1 do not classify Lack of Referential Index and Incompletely Specified Verbs as examples of deletion. Instead, they were given as examples of generalization. Later on, writers classified them as deletion phenomena. Each of these patterns can be analyzed with respect to the 4 roles of the x-bar form.

There are also about 4 different meanings for the term "operates on". The goal of this section is to coalesce them into one.

Unspecified Verb

Here's an example sentence: John gave the book to Mary.

CHAPTER 6: THE KEY LANGUAGE MODELS

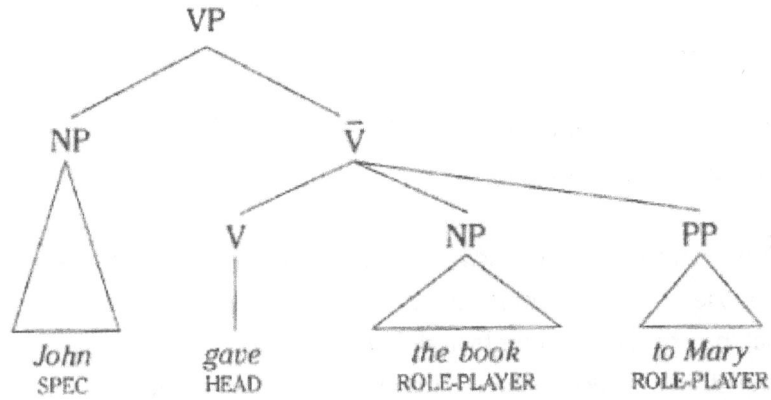

According to X-bar theory, the verb becomes the dominant force in the sentence. It also determines the kind of role-players, and how many, it expects to be surrounded by. In the above example, our verb is "gave". This implies a giver (John), the thing being given (the books), and a receiver (Mary). The choice of the verb is crucial to whatever's going on.

In terms of ordering, both structurally and lexically, the choice of the verb "operates on" all of the other Meta Model patterns in the group. When we change the verb by either refining its range, or improving its accuracy, we also affect the SPEC and all the role-players as well.

Unspecified Referential Index – in the specifier of VP

After the verb, the next important thing is the subject of the sentence, also known as the specifier or SPEC for short. Even when the subject is present, it is usually referred to, but not pointed at, or out.

In practical terms, a sentence like "John gave the book to Mary" becomes "He gave the book to Mary." This results in a sentence that does not have a meaning based in the real world.

According to Theta criterion, there should be one and only one occupant in each key role.

Theta criterion is a constraint on X-bar theory. It was originally proposed by Noam Chomsky and is used to determine the specific match between arguments and theta roles (θ-roles) in logical form. Logical Form (LF) is a level of representation that sits next to Deep Structure and Surface Structure. It was created when linguists were trying to solve the problem of quantification.

Depending on which verb we choose, the range of who or what the subject can be has been fixed. In short, the main verb operates on Lack of Referential Index. Eric Robbie recommends that Unspecified Referential Index should be Lack of Referential Index and Unspecified Verb should be Incompletely Specified Verb because SPECIFIER and specified have new, different usages.

Unspecified Referential Index – in any of the role-players

If a role-player has not been omitted or left out, it is usually replaced with either a pronoun or pronominal.

Here's an example: Jack gave it to her

The previous argument for URI is the same as this one. To gain clarity, you would simply ask something along the lines of "gave what?" or "to whom?" In terms of ordering, Unspecified Verb operates on Unspecified Referential Index.

Simple Deletion

The argument for Unspecified Verb and Unspecified Referential Index also applies here. As stated previously, the verb determines which noun phrases can be picked as role-players.

When a deletion occurs in therapy, it usually involves what's called a "state-change" verb or state-change adjectives. The stress is generally placed on the person's emotional reaction and all the detail after that is usually omitted. This typically takes the form of "I'm hurt..." or "I'm angry...".

According to Eric Robbie, since these are the verb "to-be", but a state-description adjective, the role-players involved are those which each adjective requires. Going back to the previous example, if the person says "I'm hurt", then this should be followed up with a Noun Phrase (e.g. by your action) or an S (at what you did).

Note: S stands for Sentence.

In terms of ordering, the main verb operates on any role-player.

Comparative Deletion

When the Meta Model was first introduced, Comparative Deletion was thought of as part of a larger sentence. Specifically, there was a part of the sentence that was neither visible nor audible upon first hearing or first sight.

Here's an example sentence: Diana is much better now | than she was yesterday

In this instance, the speaker was judging Diana against some basis of comparison. To challenge the utterance, you would explicitly ask for a basis of comparison. In linguistics terms, this is known as the "comparative".

Since we're using X-bar theory, we no longer need to do that and can just focus on the words used in the x-bar phrase. We can even lump together absolute adjectives (good, fine), comparative adjectives (better, happier), and superlative adjectives (best, ultimate) and call them members of the modifier class.

A distinct advantage behind doing this is that you don't have to wait for a person to use a comparative to ask them what their standards are.

Here's another example:

Person A: This is a good idea.
Person B: Good? Compared to what?

Modifiers are selected based on the X-bar item which they modify. In other words, whatever NPs acting as a SPEC or role-player(s) they're attached to. Both Unspecified Referential Index and Simple Deletion operate on any modifier that would be employed. If a role-player isn't present, you can't insert a modifier on either side of it.

Nominalization

Nominalization is a "catch-all" for any and all patterns we've discussed so far.

Here's an example sentence: We have to improve our communication.

When we break this sentence down, The question to ask is "Who is communicating what to whom? In the original sentence, there is an entire second sentence turned into a single word, and then "frozen" and tucked away inside of the first one. This means that the nominalization already contains a verb. We reveal the verb by taking the original head noun (i.e. communication) and turning it into a verb (i.e. communicating).

We also have a choice of which verb to respond to:

Choice 1: "have to" which operates on improve
Choice 2: "improve" which operates on communicating
Choice 3: communicating itself

Most accounts of the Meta Model only suggest the last.

Within the inner sentence, nominalization operates on everything else. In the outer sentence, the verb head "improves" operates on "communication".

Generalization Patterns

As the name implies, these Meta Model patterns deal with generalizing, or forming broad conclusions based on limited data.

Universal Quantifier

Sentences that begin with all/always, every/none, and every time/never, usually show in relation to people and things or with actions (i.e. how often a verb is occurring).

Here's an example sentence in relation to people: All my friends lie to me

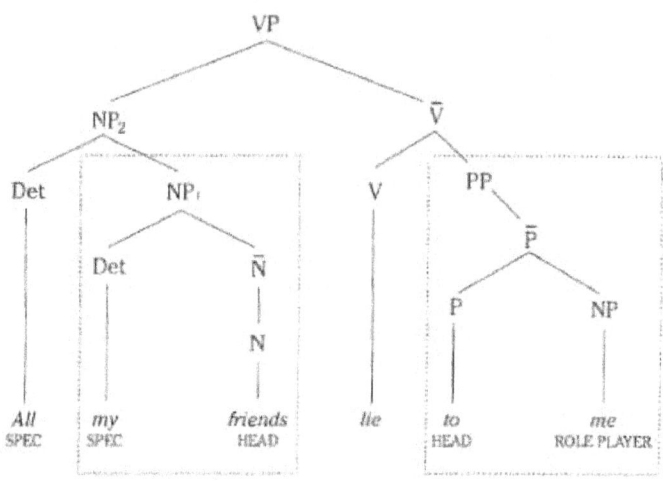

If we were to write this in standardized logic, this would have a "for all x" form which looks like the following:

For all x: if x is my friend, x lies to me

In this instance, x is a variable and could take on any value from a range.

"For all x" represents the quantifier and "if x is my friend, x lies to me" is the proposition which gets quantified.

It's important to note that the quantifier is at the "front" of the sentence in both the "natural language" version and the "professional logician" version. The word "all" affects the whole sentence.

When the Universal Quantifier is added to a verb, it tells you about actions and processes, and focuses on time instead of quantity.

Here's an example sentence (credits to Steven Pinker): Glasgow Rangers always win the League cup comfortably.

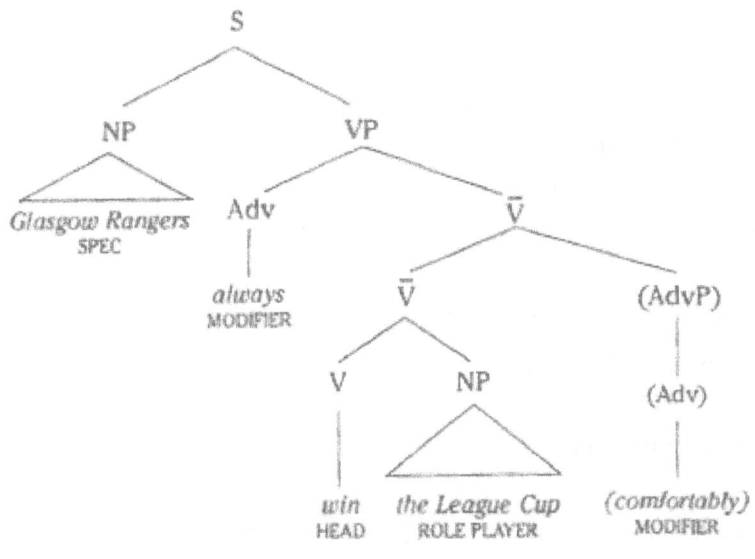

(Diagram Robbie, after Pinker)

In this example, the word "always" modifies the whole sentence.

According to Eric Robbie, the "quantifying effect" of the word always wraps itself around the VP, and then around the whole sentence.

Here's how a professional logician would phrase this sentence:

For all x: if x is (the team called) "Glasgow Rangers", x wins the Scottish League

In this instance, "for all x" not only means for every instance, but for every instance through time, or for all times.

The logical form for actions and processes is the exact same as the logical form for people and things.

The above-analysis also applies for what used to be called "Generalized Referential Index". The "referential index" refers to the subject of the sentence. GRI can be treated as if there were an implied all in front of it.

For example, the sentence "people are weird" can be read as "All people are weird".

Modal Operators

There are 2 main types of Modal Operators: possibility (can and can't) and necessity (must and mustn't).

Here's an example: The Red Sox can't win the World Series this year.

CHAPTER 6: THE KEY LANGUAGE MODELS

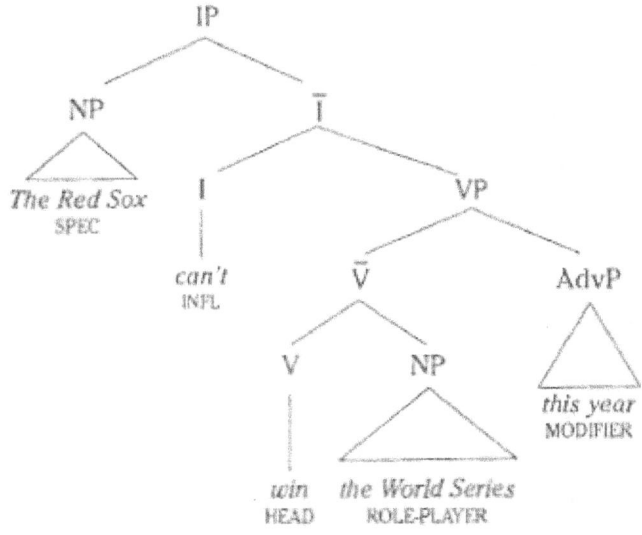

(Example based on Pinker, 1994, p.118)

In this example, "can't" starts off by operating on the VP who's head word is "win", and winds up controlling the whole sentence.

We can also show the global influence of can't by formally moving it to the front of the sentence and have it "work on" the entire proposition. The logical form of the above sentence is "not-possible p" where p stands for any proposition.

Here's how it would read according to professional logic:

(It is) not possible (that): the Red Sox will win the World Series this year

This also happens when the key word is must (or mustn't) rather than can't. You would still move the word to the front of the sentence, and the logical form of the sentence would be "necessary p" where p stands for any proposition.

Here's an example sentence: Glasgow Rangers must win the Scottish League cup

If we were to write this sentence in standardized logic, here's how that would look like:

(It is) necessary (that): Glasgow Rangers win the Scottish League cup

In conclusion, the "Generalization" patterns operate on the "Deletion" patterns.

Distortion Patterns

Distortion patterns deal with the relation between 2 sentences aka complex sentences, where you get one sentence embedded inside of the other. The outside sentence comments or reports on the "inside" one.

Lost Performative

Lost performative occurs when someone makes a rule or judgment without taking responsibility for it.

Here's an example sentence: It's bad to be inconsistent.

CHAPTER 6: THE KEY LANGUAGE MODELS

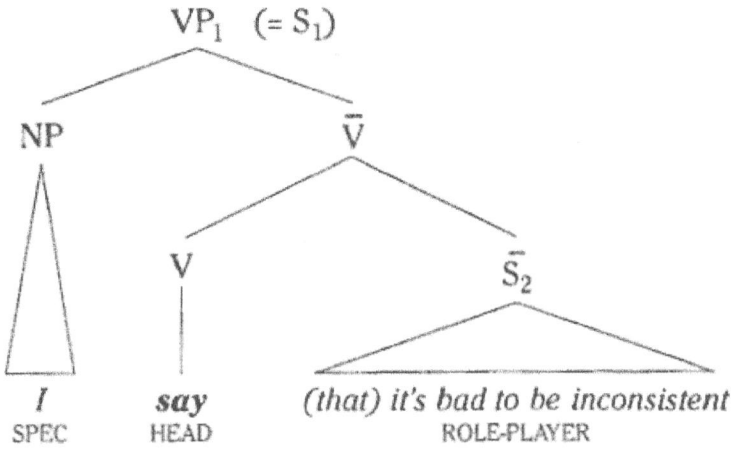

We could put it another way by saying "I say (that) it's bad to be inconsistent.

In this example, the outer sentence is "I say (that) it's bad to be inconsistent". The inner sentence is "it's bad to be inconsistent".

Note: A Verb Phrase can be generally regarded as a complete sentence.

The headword in this sentence is "say".

Mind Reading

Let's take the example sentence "You don't like me". You could put it another way by saying "I know (that) you don't like me".

For this sentence, the head word is know.

Here's a x-bar diagram to see how that looks like:

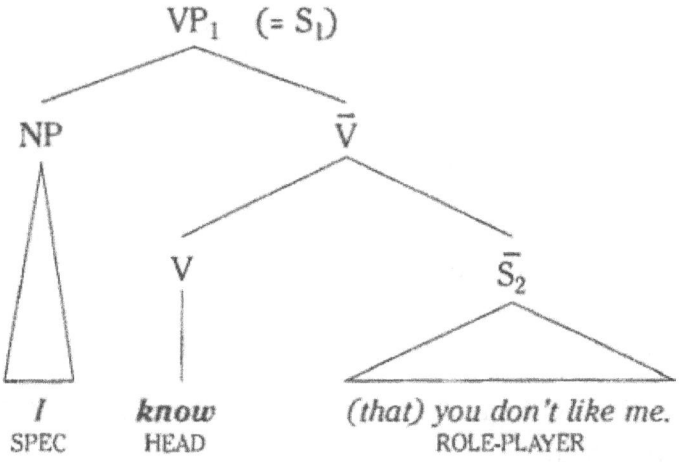

Complex Equivalence

In this pattern, the head word is "means". The subject (or SPEC) is the external evidence and what it means is an internal conclusion.

Here's an example sentence: "You don't bring me flowers means that you don't love me anymore."

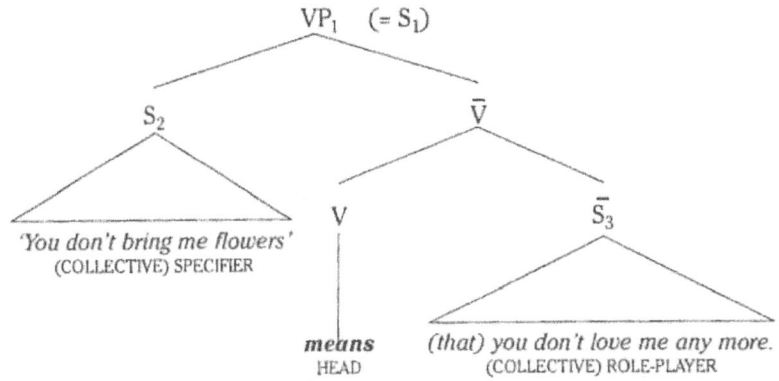

Cause & Effect

Here's an example sentence: "You make me feel bad."

In this case, "you" are the cause and "me feeling bad" is the effect. The head word for the outer sentence is "make". There's also an embedded sentence or VP, built around the second verb "feel".

Here's a diagram to illustrate this:

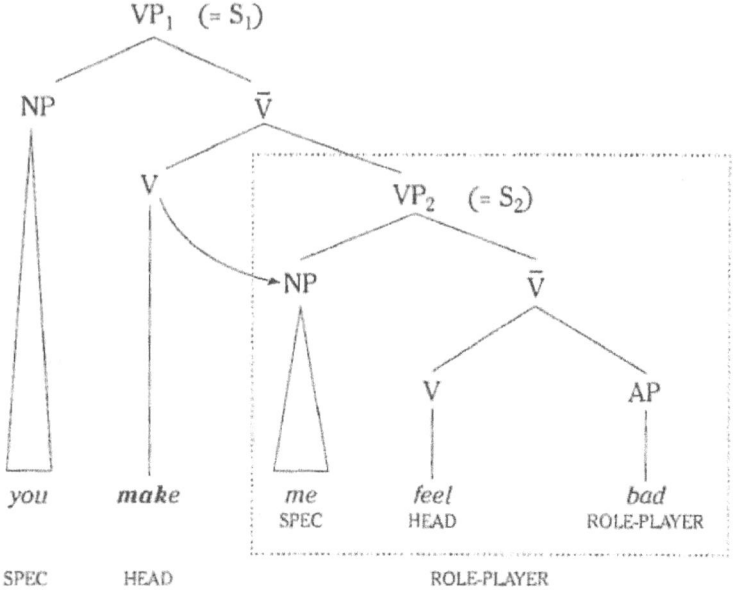

The Distortion patterns of the Meta Model all involve a shift in focus from the verb or head word inside the embedded sentence to the verb or head word of the "outside" sentence. They all involve some kind of knowledge predicate where you're either knowing or saying, or else asserting that some kind of meaning or causing is going on.

When using the words "makes" or "causes", an opinion is being formed about what's going on between the speaker and the world.

For each Distortion pattern, the head verb (aka the knowledge predicate) operates on the embedded sentence on the right. In short, the Distortion Patterns are forms of projection where the person is adding something to their map or model which isn't there in reality.

Eric Robbie recommends that we refer to the Distortion Patterns as "Addition" instead.

Presuppositions

We've saved the best one for last. And in some ways, it's the most powerful of them all.

Presuppositions operate on the rest of the Meta Model by virtue of entailment and logical form. Entailment occurs when one is able to draw necessary conclusions from a particular use of a word, phrase, or sentence.

Here's an example sentence: "If my husband knew how much I suffer, he wouldn't do that."

Given the above statement, we could ask standard Meta Model questions as follows:

- How are you suffering? (Unspecified Verb)
- What is he doing? (Simple Deletion)
- How do you know he doesn't know? (Mind Reading)
- How does his doing "that" cause you to suffer? (Cause & Effect)

When we approach it this way, we tend to get typical responses.

A better way would be to ask yourself "What must be there?" and you arrive at what's already there in her model.

Using the previous example, she could think that:

- She suffers. (Poorly Selected Verb)
- He's doing something. (Role-Player Deletion)
- He doesn't know/She knows he doesn't know. (Mind Reading)
- His doing that is causing her to suffer. (Cause & Effect)

The process of getting from what the woman said to formulating the above 4 questions is one that's taken place in your mind. This process should match what must have gone in her own mind. The act of reversing a presupposition (or multiple ones) is one of inference. You deduce, because she presupposes, the 4 statements given above, and then you respond to them.

* * *

Milton Model

Milton Erickson is widely considered to be one of the greatest Hypnotherapists that had ever lived. It's no wonder that the co-Founders of NLP, Richard Bander and John Grinder, decided to model him and figure out exactly what made him so good.

During the time that they spent learning from Milton, they started noticing a pattern in the way that he talked with his clients. It wasn't before long that they were able to formalize it, and this became known as the Milton Model.

In a nutshell, the Milton Model allows you to be "artfully vague" so that your subject can create a meaning that is appropriate for them.

So, without further ado, let's jump right into these language patterns!

Mind Reading

Much like the name implies, this language patterns claims to have the ability to know what someone else is thinking or feeling.

Examples:

I know that you're going to get a lot of value out of this blog post.

There are a lot of people just like you who feel that NLP is the world's greatest communication model.

You have seen.....(visual)

You have heard that....(auditory)

You feel that......(kinesthetic)

Lost Performative

A statement of judgment, beliefs, or standards which are expressed in such a way that the individual who has made the statement is not identified.

Examples

It is going to be a lot of fun.

It has been proven that learning NLP will lead to a richer and much more fulfilling life.

Many people think that....

It's been proven that....

All the best companies....

Cause And Effect

A statement that presupposes a one thing causing another thing to happen.

Examples:

Because you're reading this blog post on the Milton Model, you're putting yourself head and shoulders above the competition.

Reading this book to the very end allows you to feel exceptionally good about yourself.

Your being here means you're really serious about learning.

Complex Equivalence

Statements that presupposes one thing is or means the same as another thing.

Examples:

NLP is the greatest communication model in the world.

Reading this section is one of the best ways to learn the Milton Model.

Learning NLP is a good way to invest your time and energy.

Universal Quantifiers

Words that imply or state absolute conditions as being true.

Examples

Always put yourself in a state of excellence before giving a presentation.

Everyone can begin to feel totally relaxed now

Every time you begin to feel this way you can remember all the ways you change your feelings, now.

Modal Operators

Words that suggest something is necessary or possible within a person's model of the world. These include words like must, can, may, try, intend to, have to, should, able to, pretend to, ought to, etc.

Examples

NLP could be the greatest communication model in the world.

We must develop the ability to be excellent communicators.

You should consider all of the ways NLP can benefit your life.

Nominalization

Words that change a process or verb into a static event or noun. You can usually tell a word has been nominalized if it has -tion as a suffix.

Examples

A college education doesn't have the same value as it did a generation ago. (educate)

The revolution will be televised. (revolt)

There is a solution to almost every problem. (solve)

Unspecified Verbs

Verbs that do not have phrases that specify how or on what an action is performed.

Examples

At this retreat, you can begin to make many changes, starting now.

NLP can create changes in your life.

For all those reasons, you should hire our consulting firm.

Tag Questions

Questions that are used to turn the uncertainty of a question into the certainty of a statement.

(can you not?, hasn't it?, wasn't it?, aren't you?, aren't they?, can't you?, couldn't you?, don't you agree?, didn't it?)

Examples

Many people say that the Milton Model has some of the best language patterns, don't they?

That was a great movie, wasn't it?

You can see yourself using these patterns in your everyday life, can't you?

Lack of Referential Index

The use of a noun or pronoun to refer to a non specific group or category. The person doing or receiving the action is deleted.

Examples

It has been said that NLP is the greatest communication model in the world.

One can only imagine the infinite possibilities when it comes to using the Milton Model.

It is a good thing for all employees to be able to master communication skills.

Comparative Deletions

Statements that do not specifically state what or how a comparison is being made.

Examples

The best communicators in the world use NLP technology whether they know it or not

And this is more or less the right thing to do.

This is the best book on NLP.

Pacing Current Experience

Statements that describe ongoing experience.

Example

As you sit there reading this section on the Milton Model, you're beginning to realize that it's possible for you to learn these hypnotic language patterns and become a master communicator.

Double Binds

Statements that offer two or more choices that are in fact the same choice.

Examples

Are you ready to get started now or in a day or two?

You may begin to feel terrific immediately or it may take several minutes before you begin to feel great.

Would you like to go ahead and set up an appointment or should we just jot down a time when we can meet?

Conversational Postulate

A statement in the form of a question which when asked and taken literally would require a yes or no answer. This statement is normally taken as a command to perform the requested action. This works best when using the voice intonation of a command.

Examples

This is the contract; do you have a pen to sign it?

Can you run a quick errand for me?

Do you have Visa or Master card to pay for our change program?

Extend Quotes

A statement that contains one or more quotes that are intertwined with each other and with the story so that it becomes ambiguous as to what is quote and what is story

Examples

One of my clients in a firm that I worked with said that he told two people in another organization, and he told them directly Jim, you should hire my firm and that each of them said that they had been telling others to consider it seriously and he knew I could only work with a few companies right now.

I was talking to a communications expert who said one of the most respected communicators told her that NLP is the greatest communication model in the world today and that she used it always.

Selection Restriction Violation

Statements that are violations of well-formed meaning as understood by native speakers of English.

Examples

When money talks you should hire my firm to make more of it for you.

A chair can have feelings...

Embedded Commands

Statements that include indirect commands embedded within the statement itself.

Examples

When people like yourself, Jim, <u>attend my seminar</u> they get excited about how they can make many changes in their lives.

When clients <u>hire my firm</u>, Jim, all the work we do is to get results right now.

All the experts who study NLP in-depth <u>agree with me</u> that it's the world's greatest communication model

Embedded Questions

Questions that are embedded within a larger sentence.

Examples

I'm curious to know what you think about this book.

I wonder how driven you are to effectively use the Milton Model.

Covering All Ranges of Possibilities

Statements which cover all ranges of what is possible.

Examples

When you decide to write a contract with me, I can work with my associates, work with some of your internal resource people or I can come in and do the work by myself.

When you decide to buy my product, you can write a check, use your credit card or pay cash which ever is more convenient for you. I prefer to write a check, which do you prefer?

Utilization

Statements that use everything as though you control it, as though you planned it and thought of it

Example 1

Person A: I'm not sold on this product

Person B: Of course you're not sold on this seminar because I haven't told you about all of our success stories as well as the one piece of information that you need to know about before you are completely sold.

Example 2

Person A: My company is not like all those others you have worked with.

Person B: Yes, you're right, every company is different and that's exactly the reason you need to hire my firm, we tailor our services to fit your company exactly.

Example 3

Person A: There are many other great communication models.

Person B: You're right, there are many other great communication models; that is actually how NLP was able to take the best of the best to make an even better model.

Building Excitement and Expectations

Statements used to create excitement and expectation.

Examples

In a few minutes, I'm going to tell you how you can double your income with no extra work by joining my business opportunity.

In the next hour you're going to learn how to use the techniques of the greatest communication model in the world to triple your income.

In a few minutes we will explain what almost everyone says is one of the best opportunities around.

Truisms About Sensations and Time

Universal statements about sensations and time.

Examples

Most people have experienced a feeling of being totally relaxed and that's what you'll experience in one part of this comprehensive change seminar.

Most people know that it takes a long time to develop expertise on communication all by yourself; that's why they hire a firm like mine.

Sooner or later people discover that NLP is the greatest communication model in the world.

Open-ended Suggestions

Statements that do not place boundaries on what is possible or not possible in the future.

Examples

We all are capable of making more money than we do right now. My business opportunity is one way to do this.

All people have the ability to master the Milton Model, and it is much more easily achieved by reading this section.

We all have potentials that we are not aware of, and we usually don't know how they will be expressed.

Single Binds

Statements that link one cause to one effect as the only possibility.

Examples

The greater the need to improve communication, the less time you should waste before you learn the Milton Model.

The more you practice these language patterns the more you'll will be able to use them at an unconscious level.

As you continue to learn to use these tools you'll find that the more you use them they become easier and easier to use and the more you use them; the more you understand them at a deeper level.

I'm not going to Tell You...

A statement used to covertly or indirectly make an assertion.

Examples

I'm not going to tell you that the Milton Model contains powerful language patterns, I'm going to let you find that out for yourself.

I'm not going to tell you that you should hire my firm, I would be silly to tell you to hire my firm when we haven't even discussed the services you need yet.

Compound Suggestions

A statement that makes a suggestion that one would like to be accepted and covertly covers this up by making a second statement of fact.

Syntax: (1st suggestion) <then> (2nd suggest of a fact)

Example

It is to your company's advantage to hire me. How we communicate is important, isn't it?

Phonological Ambiguity

Words that sound the same but have different meanings. They're generally used to cause ambiguity when spoken.

Examples

you ewe, there their, our hour, sea see, four for, bee be, know no, knows nose, I eye, by buy bye, pray prey

* * *

Sleight of Mouth

Sleight Of Mouth is one of the classic NLP Language Patterns originally formulated by Robert Dilts.

In a book titled "Sleight Of Mouth: The Magic of Conversational Belief Change," Robert outlines 14 Language Patterns that he discovered during a training held by Richard Bandler, one of the co-founders of NLP. During this training, Richard pretends to have a "paranoid" belief system and challenged the group to change it. Despite their best efforts, they were unable to do so.

Dilts would later realize that the same language patterns that Robert was using were also used by people like Lincoln, Gandhi, Jesus and others, to "promote positive and powerful social change". By mastering these patterns, you can easily establish, shift or transform beliefs through the power of language.

With that being said, let's jump right into learning these Sleight Of Mouth language patterns.

Note: For each example, the limiting belief we will be changing is *I have had this belief for such a long time that it will be difficult to change.*

Intention

This patterns directs attention to the purpose or intention behind the belief.

Example

I very much admire and support your desire to be honest with yourself.

Positive Intention = "honesty"

Redefining

To substitute a new word for one of the words used in the belief statement that means something similar but has different implications.

Example 1

Yes, something that you've held onto so tenaciously can be quite challenging to let go of.

"had a long time" => "held onto tenaciously"

"difficult to change" => "quite challenging to let go of"

Example 2

I agree that it can initially feel pretty strange to go beyond familiar territory.

"belief" => "familiar territory"

"difficult to change" => "initially feel pretty strange"

Consequence

To direct attention to an effect (either positive or negative) of the belief, or the generalization defined by the belief, which changes (or reinforces) the belief.

Examples

When you expect something will be difficult, it will seem that much easier when you finally do it.

Genuinely acknowledging our concerns allows us to set them aside so we can focus on what matters.

Chunk Down

Breaking the elements of the belief into smaller pieces that changes (or reinforces) the generalization defined by the belief.

Examples

Since having this belief only a short time would make it easier to change, perhaps you can remember what it was like back at the time when you had just formed the belief and imagine having changed it at that time.

"long time" => "short time"

Perhaps if, instead of trying to change the whole belief at once, if you just altered it in small increments, it would seem easy and fun.

"changing a belief" => "altering it in increments"

Chunk Up

Generalizing an element of the belief to a larger classification that changes (or reinforces) the relationship defined by the belief.

Example

The past does not always accurately predict the future. Knowledge can evolve rapidly when it is reconnected with the processes which naturally update it.

"had for a long time" => "past"

"belief" => "a form of knowledge"

"change" => "connected with the natural processes which naturally update it"

Analogy

Finding a relationship analogous to that defined by the belief which challenges (or reinforces) the generalization defined by the belief.

Examples

A belief is like a law. Even very old laws can be changed quickly if enough people vote for something new.

A belief is like a computer program. The issue is not how old the program is, it's whether or not you know the programming language.

Change Frame Size

Re-evaluating (or reinforcing) the implication of the belief in the context of a longer (or shorter) time frame, a larger number of people (or from an individual point of view) or a bigger or smaller perspective.

Examples

In a couple of years from now, you will probably have difficulty remembering that you ever had this belief.

I'm sure that your future kids will appreciate the fact that you made the effort to change this belief, rather than passing it on to them.

Another Outcome

Switching to a different goal other than the one addressed or implied by the belief, in order to challenge (or reinforce) the relevancy of the belief.

Examples

It's not necessary to change the belief. It just needs to be updated.

The problem isn't so much about changing beliefs. It's about making your map of the world congruent with who you are now.

Model Of The World

Re-evaluating (or reinforcing) the belief from the framework of a different model of the world.

Examples

You're lucky. Most people don't even recognize that their limitations are a function of their beliefs that can be changed at all. You're doing a lot better than the average person.

Artists are known to use their inner struggles as a source of inspiration for creativity. I wonder what type of creativity your efforts to change your belief might bring out in you.

Reality Strategy

Re-evaluating (or reinforcing) the belief accounting for the fact that people operate from their cognitive perceptions of the world in order to build their beliefs.

Examples

How, specifically do you know that you have had this belief for a 'long time'?

What particular qualities of what you see or hear when you think about changing this belief make it seem 'difficult'?"

Counterexample

Finding an example that challenges or enriches the generalization defined by the belief.

Example

I have seen many beliefs established and changed instantaneously when people are provided with the appropriate experiences and support.

Hierarchy of Criteria

Re-evaluating (or reinforcing) the belief according to a criterion that is addressed that is more important than any addressed by the belief.

Examples

The degree to which a belief fits with and supports one's vision and mission is more important than how long one has had the belief.

Personal congruence and integrity are worth whatever effort it takes to achieve them.

Apply to Self

Evaluating the belief statement itself according to the relationship or criteria defined by the belief.

Examples

How long have you held the opinion that the difficulty in changing beliefs is primarily a matter of time?

How difficult do you think it would be to change your belief that long held generalizations are difficult to change?

Meta Frame

Evaluating the belief from the frame of an ongoing, personally oriented context. In other words, establishing a belief about the belief.

Examples

Perhaps you have the belief that beliefs are difficult to change, because you have previously lacked the tools and understanding necessary to change them easily.

Chapter 7: NLP Anchoring

Anchoring Fundamentals

Anchoring is a powerful technique in NLP that allows you to access any desired state of mind at will. By creating an association between a specific stimulus and a specific experience, you can trigger that experience whenever you want by activating the stimulus. This can help you enhance your performance, overcome challenges, and achieve your goals.

Anchoring is often misunderstood as a simple stimulus-response mechanism, like the one demonstrated by Pavlov's famous experiment with dogs. In that experiment, Pavlov conditioned the dogs to salivate whenever they heard a bell ringing, by repeatedly presenting them with food at the same time as the bell. The bell became a stimulus that elicited a response of salivation, even without the presence of food.

However, anchoring is more than just a stimulus-response mechanism. It is based on the principle that every experience is composed of multiple sensory modalities, such as visual, auditory, kinesthetic, olfactory, and gustatory. These modalities form a complex pattern or gestalt that represents the experience in our mind. When we recall an experience, we activate some or all of these modalities, depending on how vivid and detailed our memory is.

Anchoring works by linking a specific stimulus to a specific modality or a combination of modalities that represent the desired experience. The stimulus can be anything that is unique and easy to reproduce, such as a word, a gesture, a sound, a smell, or a touch. The experience can be anything that is meaningful and relevant to you, such as a feeling of confidence, happiness, calmness, or motivation.

There are two types of anchors: natural and artificial. Natural anchors are stimuli that are already associated with certain experiences, either by coincidence or by repetition. For example, a song that reminds you of a happy moment, a perfume that reminds you of a loved one, or a place that reminds you of a relaxing vacation. Natural anchors can be used to trigger positive experiences that can help you in different situations.

Artificial anchors are stimuli that are deliberately created and linked to certain experiences, either by yourself or by someone else. For example, you can create an anchor for confidence by squeezing your fist while recalling a time when you felt confident, or you can create an anchor for relaxation by touching your earlobe while recalling a time when you felt relaxed. Artificial anchors can be customized and tailored to your specific needs and goals.

The effectiveness of anchoring depends on several factors, such as the intensity of the experience, the uniqueness of the stimulus, the timing of the association, and the frequency of the reinforcement. The more intense the experience, the more unique the stimulus, the more precise the timing, and the more frequent the reinforcement, the stronger and more reliable the anchor will be.

* * *

State Elicitation

State elicitation is the process of bringing yourself or someone else into a specific emotional or mental state. It involves accessing a memory or an imagination that is associated with that state, and then amplifying it by using your senses, your language, and your physiology.

State elicitation is not only essential for anchoring, but also for any other NLP technique that requires a change of state, such as reframing, sub-modalities, or parts integration. It is also a valuable skill for communication, persuasion, and rapport building, as it allows you to match and influence the states of others.

Here are some guidelines for effective state elicitation:

- Start with yourself. Before you can elicit a state in someone else, you need to be able to elicit it in yourself. This means that you need to have a rich and varied repertoire of states that you can access at will. The more states you can experience, the more states you can elicit in others. To expand your range of states, you can use NLP modeling, which we covered in a previous section, to copy the

structure of excellence from someone who has the state that you want.
- Pay attention to your physiology. Your physiology is the key to your state. How you breathe, how you move, how you hold your posture, how you use your facial expressions, all affect how you feel. If you want to elicit a positive state, you need to adopt a physiology that matches that state. For example, if you want to elicit confidence, you need to stand tall, breathe deeply, smile, and look ahead. Conversely, if you want to elicit a negative state, you need to adopt a physiology that matches that state. For example, if you want to elicit fear, you need to shrink, breathe shallowly, frown, and look down.
- Pay attention to your blood sugar. Your blood sugar level is another factor that influences your state. If your blood sugar is too low or too high, you will have difficulty controlling your state. You may feel tired, irritable, anxious, or depressed. To maintain a balanced blood sugar level, you need to eat healthy foods, avoid processed sugars, and drink plenty of water.
- Use your language evocatively. Your language is another powerful tool for state elicitation. The words you use, the tone you use, the metaphors you use, all have an impact on how you and others feel. If you want to elicit a strong state, you need to use language that is vivid, sensory, and emotional. For example, if you want to elicit excitement, you can say "Imagine that you are on a roller coaster, feeling the wind in your hair, the adrenaline in your veins, and the thrill in your heart" If you want to elicit a weak state, you need to use language that is vague, abstract, and neutral. For example, if you want to elicit boredom, you can say "Think about something that is not very interesting, like a routine task, a dull lecture, or a boring conversation".
- Be willing to be flexible. One of the most important principles of

NLP is flexibility. This means that you need to be able to adapt to different situations, different people, and different outcomes. When it comes to state elicitation, you need to be willing to try different approaches, different stimuli, and different anchors, until you find what works best for you and your clients. You also need to be willing to set aside your own personal biases, preferences, and limitations, and focus on what serves the purpose of the interaction. For example, if you are working with a client who wants to overcome a phobia, you may need to elicit a state of fear in them, even if you don't like feeling fear yourself.

- Ask yourself these 2 questions. Before you elicit a state in someone else, you need to have a clear idea of what state you want to elicit, and why. To do that, you can ask yourself 2 questions: What kinds of states do I want to elicit from people? and What kinds of states would be useful to draw out for the outcomes I have with my clients? These questions will help you to choose the most appropriate and effective states for your goals.

* * *

Stacking Anchors vs. Chaining Anchors

Chaining anchors is a technique that allows you to guide someone from their present state to a desired state, by using a series of intermediate states that are linked by anchors. Anchors are stimuli that trigger a specific state or response in someone. For example, a song can be an anchor for a happy state, or a gesture can be an anchor for a confident state.

To use chaining anchors, follow these steps:

1. Identify the present state and the desired state of the person you want to influence. For example, if you want to help someone overcome their fear of public speaking, their present state might be anxious and their desired state might be confident.

1. Identify a few intermediate states that can bridge the gap between the present state and the desired state. These states should be logically and emotionally connected, and each one should be closer to the desired state than the previous one. For example, some intermediate states between anxious and confident might be calm, relaxed, curious, and interested.
2. Anchor each state with a unique stimulus, such as a word, a touch, a sound, or a gesture. Make sure that the stimulus is distinctive and consistent for each state. For example, you could use each knuckle on a person's hand for each intermediate state.
3. Test each anchor to make sure that it elicits the intended state in the person. To do this, fire the anchor and observe the person's response. If the anchor works, you should see a change in their physiology, such as their breathing, posture, facial expression, or tone of voice. If the anchor does not work, you may need to repeat the anchoring process or choose a different stimulus.
4. Chain the anchors together by firing them in sequence, starting from the present state and moving towards the desired state. As

you do this, you should notice that the person's state changes accordingly. For example, you can touch the first knuckle for calm, the second knuckle for relaxed, the third knuckle for curious, and then the last knuckle to elicit interested. By the time you reach the last anchor, the person should be in the desired state of confident.
5. The purpose of chaining anchors is to teach the person how to access the desired state on their own, whenever they need it. To do this, you need to transfer the final anchor to the person, so that they can use it as a trigger for the desired state. For example, you can teach the person to touch their knuckle whenever they want to feel confident. This way, they can use the knuckle as a shortcut to access the state of confidence, without going through the whole chain of anchors.

Stacking anchors is a technique that allows you to enhance the intensity and quality of a desired state, by combining multiple states that are associated with the same anchor. For example, if you want to create a powerful state of motivation, you can stack multiple states that contribute to motivation, such as passion, excitement, determination, and enthusiasm.

To use stacking anchors, you need to follow these steps:

1. Identify the desired state and the anchor that you want to use for it. The anchor can be any stimulus that is easy to reproduce and control, such as a word, a touch, a sound, or a gesture. For example, if you want to create a state of motivation, you can use your earlobe as the anchor.

2. Identify a few states that are related to the desired state and that can amplify it. These states should be positive, congruent, and complementary to the desired state. For example, some states that are related to motivation are passion, excitement, determination, and enthusiasm.
3. Anchor each state with the same stimulus that you chose for the desired state. To do this, you need to elicit each state in the person, either by asking them to recall a time when they felt that state, or by using another anchor that is already linked to that state. Then, apply the stimulus as the peak of the state. For example, you can ask the person to remember a time when they felt passionate about something, and then have them touch their earlobe as they're fully immersed in the state of passion. Repeat this process for each state that you want to stack.
4. Test the anchor to make sure that it elicits the desired state and all the stacked states in the person. To do this, fire the anchor and observe the person's response. If the anchor works, you should see a change in their physiology, such as their breathing, posture, facial expression, or tone of voice. If the anchor does not work, you may need to repeat the anchoring process or choose a different stimulus.
5. Stack the anchor by firing it repeatedly, each time adding more intensity and duration to the stimulus. As you do this, you should notice that the person's state becomes stronger and more robust. For example, you can have them touch their earlobe once, then twice, then three times, each time a little longer. By the time they reach the last repetition, the person should be in a powerful state of motivation.
6. The purpose of stacking anchors is to create a state that is more resilient and resourceful, and that can help the person achieve their goals. To do this, you need to link the anchor to the specific

context or situation where the person wants to use the state. For example, you can ask the person to imagine themselves in a scenario where they need to be motivated, and then fire the anchor to activate the state of motivation. This way, they can use the anchor as a tool to access the state of motivation, whenever they face a challenge or an opportunity.

* * *

How to Use Anchoring in Persuasion

In NLP, we use anchoring to elicit and transfer emotional states, beliefs, and behaviors from one context to another. However, we can also use anchoring for persuasion, as well as for personal change and growth.

Anchoring is not a manipulative tool that you can use to control people's minds. It is a collaborative process that requires rapport, trust, and respect. You cannot anchor someone without their permission and cooperation. Anchoring is based on the principle of ecology, which means that any change you make should be beneficial for yourself and others, and not cause any harm or conflict.

There are many ways to use anchoring in persuasion, depending on your purpose and the situation. Here are some general guidelines that can help you apply anchoring effectively:

- First, you need to establish rapport with the person you want to persuade. Rapport is the feeling of connection and harmony that makes communication easier and more enjoyable. You can build rapport by matching and mirroring the other person's body language, voice, words, and breathing. You can also use compliments, humor, and common interests to create rapport.

- Next, you need to identify the state or outcome that you want the other person to experience or achieve. This could be a positive emotion, a belief, a value, or a behavior that is relevant to your topic or goal. For example, if you want to persuade someone to buy your product, you might want them to feel confident, curious, or satisfied. If you want to persuade someone to join your cause, you might want them to feel passionate, inspired, or committed.

- Then, you need to elicit the state or outcome in the other person, by using questions, stories, metaphors, or examples that relate to their experience and interests. You can also use sensory language, such as visual, auditory, kinesthetic, olfactory, or gustatory words, to appeal to their senses and imagination. For example, if you want to elicit curiosity, you might say something like "Imagine what it would be like to..." or "Have you ever wondered how...". If you want to elicit satisfaction, you might say something like "Think of a time when you felt really satisfied with something you did or bought..." or "How would you feel if you had...".

- As you elicit the state or outcome, you need to anchor it to a specific stimulus, such as a word, a gesture, a touch, a sound, or an image. The stimulus should be unique, distinctive, and easy to reproduce. You should also anchor the state or outcome at its peak, when it is the most intense and vivid. To anchor the state or outcome, you need to present the stimulus at the same time as the state or outcome is elicited, and repeat it several times to strengthen the association. For example, if you want to anchor confidence, you might say the word "confidence" in a confident tone, or make a thumbs-up gesture, or touch the other person's shoulder, as they are feeling confident.

- Finally, you need to test and fire the anchor, to make sure that it works and that it triggers the desired state or outcome. To test the anchor, you need to break the state or outcome, by changing the topic or asking a neutral question, and then present the stimulus again, to see if the state or outcome is reactivated. To fire the anchor, you need to present the stimulus at the appropriate moment, when you want the other person to experience or achieve the state or outcome. For example, if you want to fire the confidence anchor, you might say the word "confidence" or make the gesture or touch, as you are asking the other person to buy your product or join your cause.

By using anchoring in persuasion, you can help the other person feel more positive, motivated, and aligned with your message or goal. You can also help yourself feel more confident, persuasive, and influential. Anchoring is a skill that you can practice and improve over time, by observing and learning from others, and by experimenting and getting feedback. Remember to use anchoring ethically and responsibly, and to respect the other person's choice and free will. Anchoring is not a magic trick, but a way of enhancing communication and connection.

NLP Anchoring Best Practices

To create effective anchors, you need to follow a few best practices. One of them is to have a clear TOTE model in mind. TOTE stands for Test-Operate-Test-Exit, and it is a feedback loop that guides your actions and decisions.

The TOTE model helps you to:

- Test the current state of yourself or your client, and compare it to the desired state.
- Operate on the state by applying an intervention, such as an anchor, a reframing, or a sub-modality shift.
- Test the state again, and evaluate the results of the intervention. Did it move you closer to the desired state, or further away from it?
- Exit the loop if the desired state is achieved, or repeat the process if not.

The TOTE model is not a rigid formula, but a flexible framework that adapts to the situation and the person.

It's important to remember that the step-by-step procedures you can learn in a training or in a book are not how you work with people. They're how you learn. When working with people, the most important thing is how you relate to them. Rapport is the foundation of any successful NLP intervention. Sometimes, the best work you do with your clients happens before the session even starts, when you establish trust and understanding.

Communication is like a "dance" between two people, and you need to be able to alter what you're doing when the time calls for it. Michael Breen once said that NLPers act as "refined feedback machines". We pay attention to the verbal and non-verbal cues of our clients, and we adjust our questions and responses accordingly. The purpose of asking questions is to get people to go into their own experience, and to elicit the information we need to create effective anchors.

Some questions we can ask include:

- What state do you want to anchor?
- When was the last time you felt that state?
- How do you know when you are in that state?
- What do you see, hear, and feel when you are in that state?
- How do you want to trigger that state?

Once you've worked with enough people, you'll notice that there are only a handful of patterns and strategies you need to be aware of. It's your job to find them, and to use them to your advantage. One of the patterns you need to be aware of is the timing of the anchor. Many people worry about getting this right, but there isn't a one-size-fits-all solution.

The best way to time an anchor is to get good at observing other people. Everyone is different. Some people reach the peak of their state quickly and drop out. For other people, the state builds up gradually and lasts longer. You need to calibrate your anchor to the person's physiology, and to the intensity and duration of their state. The general rule is to fire the anchor when the state is at its highest point, and to release it before it starts to fade.

Chapter 8: Meta-States

What are Meta-States?

A Meta-State is a state of consciousness that is above or beyond another state and which is about that other state of awareness. The word "meta" indicates a higher level. It refers to something that is above, beyond, or about something else.

In meta-communication, we communicate about communicating. In meta-feeling, we experience a feeling state about a feeling. In meta-analysis, we take a step back and look at several analyses and try to find a pattern.

When you bring a higher state to a lower one, the higher one contains the lower one. The lower one becomes a member of the class set of the higher one. It's a fundamental principle in Meta-States that higher levels govern lower levels.

For example, if you bring excitement to your learning, then excitement becomes the classification or category for learning. Learning becomes a member class of things that make you excited.

To understand Meta-States, it's important to note the difference between meta-states and primary states. When you're in a primary state, you're focused on the outside environment and you have thoughts-and-feelings about what's happening around you. When you go meta, you go above your primary thoughts-and-feelings and start having thoughts-and-feelings about your primary experience.

A meta-state always begins with a thought-and-feeling about a primary state. From there, we can layer multiple levels of thoughts and emotions. Meta-States can be emotions, thoughts, or somatic experiences. It's a dynamic complex of the entire mind-body-emotion system.

Since emotions play such a critical part in our overall state, it helps to understand what they are and how they arise. A state is always an emotional state and is not static as the name suggests. States are dynamic and constantly in flux.

Emotions are always relative to thinking and experiencing. They arise because they weigh the difference between expectation and reality. If reality is greater than expectations, then we're happy. If our expectation is greater than reality, then we become sad or frustrated.

CHAPTER 8: META-STATES

Credit: *travelthewholeworld.org*

Because of the way that emotions work, they're not a reliable indicator for determining what's real or what's good for you. They can only tell you about the relationship between your mental mapping and sensory experience. The accuracy of your emotions can also be greatly diminished if you have a distorted model of the world.

Meta-States is partially inspired by General Semantics from Alfred Korzybski. Korzybski also discusses concepts related to Meta-States in his book "Science And Sanity". In his book, he uses the term "second-order states" which behaves similarly to Meta-States.

According to him, there are some states which will negate the effects of another state and create a positive effect. For example, inhibition of inhibition becomes a positive release, hate of hate is close to love, and doubt of doubt becomes scientific criticism.

Crash Course on States

I've talked about states briefly in the previous section, but it's an entire subject on its own. The topic of state originates from the field of psychology. William James, the father of American Psychology, spoke extensively about states.

Our states are Neuro-linguistic states, states of mind-and-body that we experience primarily as an emotional state.

Most people don't refer to their states as "states". We tend to use different names like attitude, mood, or emotions. Whether you realize it or not, you're always in a state. We always operate out of some state and our lives are a composite of our mental and emotional state.

States are highly dynamic and are always changing. As a mental state, it involves whatever is in your mind at a given moment. As an emotional state, it involves what you're presently feeling. As a physiological state, it involves the condition of your mind and body.

States embody all of these things simultaneously, which is why they are so dynamic, full of energy, holistic, and nonlinear i.e. systemic.

States can also be described as an energy field. When you're in a state, you experience mental energy, emotional energy, and physiological energy. They encompass the energy you expend in thinking, emoting, behaving, speaking, etc. and they create the energies that make up your experiential state.

Because states describe your physical energy field, you can feel them. This is why we can "feel" the states of other people. We can feel other people's sadness, excitement, fear, etc. You can also feel the energy of someone's state in their breath, movement, voice, gesture, etc.

Your state is the result of what and how you communicate to yourself about the things happening around you. What and how you map what you see, feel, and hear, through your representational systems and how you map the meanings you attribute to what you've mapped becomes your inner reality. This mapping operates as your model of the world.

Your experience of reality is not a function of the world "out there" but a function of what and how you mapped your reality. We can therefore conclude that the main factor in your life is not your DNA, parents, the economy, or any other external factor but what and how you map the territory.

We must treat our maps as tools and not become overly attached to them. A map is only useful to the extent that it can take you from Point A to Point B. This is why Alfred Korzybski said, "The map is not the territory".

If you want to understand your internal map better, ask yourself the following questions:

- How do you represent the outside world?

- What representational systems do you use?
- What is the quality of the sensory map you use?
- What is the quality of your linguistic maps?

Your map can put you in different mind-body states.

The way we communicate with ourselves will reflect in our emotional state. For example, if you're in a joyful state, then you're probably going to be thinking joyful thoughts. When you're sad, you have sad thoughts.

We can access a particular state by using either our mind or body. Knowing this gives us the ability to work more precisely with states.

Let's say you wanted to access the state of confidence. If you wanted to go the mind route, you can say "What are you thinking right now that creates the confidence you're feeling?" If you were to go the feeling route, you can say "What's the most effective way for you to use your body to feel confident?"

State management involves being able to take charge of running the content and processes in your brain. These content and processes include your internal representations such as sights, sounds, feelings, smells and immediate sensory experience. It also includes words and language forms that make up your beliefs, values, understandings, etc.

States also include your perceptual filters and meta-programs. These lie outside of conscious awareness and govern what you pay attention to.

CHAPTER 8: META-STATES

As you internally represent ideas, understandings, beliefs, and so on, you supply the contents of your mind-body state. You become inwardly formed and shaped by your sights, sounds, sensations, and language.

The quality of your states determine the quality of your life. You can only become your best self by getting into the right state.

Your states reflect your consciousness and your consciousness generates, induces, and creates states. Not only does your consciousness creates your states, but once you're in state, the state determines or strongly influences your consciousness.

As we change states, our experience changes as well. Our thinking, perceiving, remembering, learning, etc. changes to correspond to the state. And all of this functions as a loop.

State and consciousness work together to affect and influence one another. They feed each other. The more you get into a stressed-out state, the more stressed-out you become. The more you get into a relaxed state, the more relaxed you become. This goes to show that if you don't take control of your states, they will control you.

If you manage your states in a positive direction, then you can build upon your strengths and amplify your existing resources as well as create new ones.

To manage your mind in accessing empowering and resourceful states, you need the ability to interrupt disempowering and unresourceful states. This is easier than you think. Partly because we interrupt states all the time.

Have you ever been in the middle of something and then your phone rings out of nowhere? That's an example of a state interrupt.

By having a good number of state interrupts, you give yourself the ability to manage your consciousness and prevent your states from throwing you into a negative spiral.

Consciousness gives us the ability to use our minds as an evaluator. You can step back from whatever level of consciousness, step up to the next level, and evaluate the previous level in terms of quality. At this level, we can evaluate our primary states and quality control our mind-body systems.

To quality control your states, ask yourself a variety of ecology questions such as the following:

- Is my state productive or unproductive?
- Do I find my current state useful or unuseful?
- Is my state enhancing or unenhancing?
- Empowering or disempowering?
- Does my state feel resource or unresourceful?

In every domain of your life, your ability to manage your states plays an essential role in mastery and responsibility.

It might seem like external stimuli whether it's other people, events, words, etc. cause our states but they do not. Meaning causes and determines your states as consciousness reflects your states. This is why the same event can happen to different people and each one has a different response.

Let's imagine 3 people who were working at the same company and all of them lost their job on the same day.

Person A says "I'm no good at anything".

Person B says "I should've worked harder."

Person C says "Life is so unfair".

To become aware of the presence, nature, and functioning of your state, you must first identify your state.

Here are some questions to help you identify your state:

- What is your present state?
- How did you get into that state?
- What are the contributing factors of that state?

According to the Meta-States Model, there are 3 kinds of states: primary states, meta-states and gestalt states. Primary states exist at the first level of experience. Meta-states include all states at higher logical levels compared to primary states. Gestalt states are a series of meta-states that interact with one another which gives rise to richer and more complex states.

Every human experience begins as a primary state. Primary states give rise to all of the higher meta-states. Depending on who you ask, there are anywhere between 12 and 30 primary states.

Primary states tend to have a direct reference to the world "out there". These tend to be the purest experiences and are characterized by their intensity, directness, and simplicity. Because we experience those primary states so directly, they are easy to anchor. We can link them to some other stimuli whether it's a sound, word, smell, etc. so that when we trigger the linked stimuli, the state will also retrigger.

Fear is a typical example of a primary state. It has to do with some real or perceived danger on the outside. Sadness is another typical example. It involves the perception of loss and thus triggers feelings of loss.

Primary states are governed by our sensory-based representational systems such as what we see, feel, hear, etc. Our states are often driven by specific sounds, pictures, words, and/or sensations.

Sometimes the emotion of an experience is so strong that it becomes linked with a primary emotion like anger, fear, relaxation, etc. that the experience or just part of it can retrigger the state. For example, if someone has a fear of spiders and you show them a stuffed animal of a spider, they start panicking almost instantly.

Primary states are often experienced in "first position". We see, feel, and hear the information as if we're inside the "movie".

Your states operate as your frame-of-mind. They color your perception, learning, memory, behaving, etc. This is why we think, perceive, feel, etc. in accordance with our states. For instance, when we're in a learning state, we become curious and open-minded.

When you repeatedly experience a thought, feeling, or emotion, it habituates. We create habits of speech, mind, emotion, and behavior. At some point, the process by which you generate the states drops out of conscious awareness. When it becomes automatic or fast, that's what allows you to "fly into a state".

Experiencing and re-experiencing a state streamlines the accessing part. Mental and physical cues enable you to get into a state almost instantly and without thinking about it. It becomes one of your unconscious competencies. It becomes a frame of reference which gives you an internal context to access that state readily.

* * *

Beyond Primary States

At the higher levels meta to our primary states, we experience second-level, third-level, and so on, of mind and emotions. These states involve multi-layered and complex emotions like self-esteem, self-contempt, resilience, grit, etc. These are conceptual and semantic states.

In meta-states, your thoughts and emotions relate to something internal rather than "out there" like with primary states. We are interacting with our states of consciousness. In essence, you are responding to your responses.

Think about a time when you were afraid to speak up.

Ask yourself "How do you feel about that experience?" That's a meta-question. You move to a meta-level of awareness, feeling, and experiencing.

Meta-levels are a level above another level and it has a reference to the one below it. As this meta-relationship emerges, the higher inevitably affects the lower as it organizes and drives it. Because of this, meta-states can have a wide range of effects on lower states whether it's amplifying the original state, reversing it, transforming it, etc.

Meta-states involve several pieces, or even multiple pieces, of awareness and emotions. They may even involve many layers of consciousness about consciousness.

Our self-reflexive consciousness is what gives us the ability to create meta-states. Self-reflexive means that our consciousness can reflect back onto its own processes and products. In other words, after we say, think, or feel something, we can reflect on those responses and think, feel, and say about our initial responses. You are now responding to your earlier responses. It's possible to layer states upon states indefinitely.

Reflexivity leads to meta-thinking, meta-communicating, meta-feelings, meta-modeling, and meta-analyzing. Our ability to meta-state allows us to transcend time, space, being, values, and experiences. Our ability to transcend is what allows us to call experiences existential, ontological, and spiritual.

We have the ability to create all kinds of meta-states whether they're simple, complex, congruent, incongruent, gestalt states, etc. As you think and emote at meta-levels, your state of mind becomes more complex.

When we meta-state resourcefully, we can creates states of genius, flow, and self-actualization. When we meta-state unresourcefully, we create states of limitation, diseases, and all sorts of human evils. They become self-destructive because we are turning our energy against ourselves.

Meta-states tend to be less kinesthetic compared to primary states, but there are exceptions. Feelings you experience at meta-levels tend to take on a more conceptual quality. As a general rule, your meta-feelings are more cognitively informed than your raw kinesthetic feelings.

* * *

Texturing States

You can design the quality of your life by texturing the quality of your states. States are just states until you meta-state them with various qualities, resources, limitations, etc. After that, they become rich and complex states.

Our higher-level states tend to coalesce into our primary states such that we experience them as one state. The coalescing process incorporates higher-level concepts and abstractions into the primary state. What was just a mental awareness becomes embodied within your neural pathways and becomes part of your physiology.

Although our states are holistic in nature, we can tease out the higher levels to identify its component elements. We can find these levels by asking questions about the quality of our states.

Here are some example questions:

- When you get angry, what's the quality of your anger?
- Are you respectful or thoughtful when angry?
- Do you become impatient and insulting when angry?

The answers and responses that emerge from these questions flush out the higher-level frames that currently texture your state.

You can also ask other meta-level phenomena such as the following:

- What do you believe about happiness?
- What moral judgments do you make about this?
- How does anger play or fail to play into your destiny, mission, and/or vision?
- What do you expect about anger?

Through our everyday experiences, we have been qualifying our states by setting them inside frames-of-references. Each time we set a frame inside a frame-of-reference, we create another meta-state.

Higher states classify lower states. The lower state functions as a member of the class which the meta-state creates. This is why fear of anger and respect for our anger have 2 very different textures.

The mental and emotional frames we bring to our experiences represent the main governing influence in our lives. Your meta-states are all of your beliefs, values, expectations, etc.

Research Scientist Arthur Koestler created the term holon to describe reality as "whole/parts". Holons describe any entity which is whole unto itself and is simultaneously a part of another whole.

L. Michael Hall suggests thinking of states and textures as holons. We experience our states as wholes but each state exists as part of some larger whole. After state, the next larger whole is neurology which includes our brain, nervous system, life, etc.

Ken Wilber, an American philosopher, describes holons in terms of 2 factors: agency and communion, and transcendence and dissolution. Each holon has its own identity or autonomy, but since the holon is part of a larger whole, it also communicates with the larger system, which would mean it communicates with other wholes. The holon structure allows us to transcend any state or meta-state and to go beyond what we have been to become more of what we can be. We can add new components to our layers of state or we can take it apart completely.

When a holon moves up and experiences a transcendence of self, something new emerges. This can happen when you develop a compelling outcome that allows you to boldly face your fears, which creates the gestalt state of courage. Even though the state of fear is contained within the higher state, the continuous process creates discontinuities. It's a discontinuous change rather than a continuous one that would be building upon what came before. The new gestalt becomes "more than the sum of its parts".

Lower states are contained in higher ones, but higher ones are not necessarily contained in lower ones. For example, molecules contain atoms, but atoms don't contain molecules.

The mind-to-muscle process helps to create a mind-body integration which allows higher levels to texture the lower levels. This paves the way for working with layers of thoughts and states as a holon structure.

The Anatomy of Meta-States

When it comes to working with meta-states, there are a number of different features you need to keep in mind in order to utilize them effectively. There are 9 major features in total and we'll go over each one in no particular order.

Structural Complexity

Meta-states have structural complexity that arises from the layeredness of thought upon thought, feeling upon feeling, concept upon concept, etc. From this layeredness, we experience our meta-states as textured with other variables. Some of these variables are from specific thoughts and emotions we add while others are emergent properties of the system.

Kinesthetic Texturing

Meta-states generally lack strong and driving kinesthetic sensations that we experience in primary states.

Primary states involve experiencing primary emotions like fear, joy, anger, sadness, etc. It's usually easy to access the feeling experience and how they feel in your body and where in the body you experience them.

Anchoring Artistry

Meta-States cannot be anchored in the same way as primary states due to the fact that they're not kinesthetically driven. Unlike anchoring primary states, which involve linking a sensory stimulus to certain thoughts-and-feelings, anchoring meta-states involves setting up a link between one internal response and another internal response.

When we anchor a meta-state, the higher level tends to be more cerebral and intellectual in nature. As a result, there's usually less energy in the meta-state, therefore anchoring the meta-state to the first state requires more finesse.

Despite these downsides, it's still possible to anchor meta-states and we can do them in any of the representational systems.

If you want a meta-state anchor to take hold, it's important to solidify the meta-state through questioning, rehearsal, and feedback summaries. When you're working with another person, you will need to keep reflecting the words, ideas, and meanings that will help the person find the right words and symbols for them. The right words and symbols will help integrate the conceptual meanings and understandings of the meta-state.

It's also a good idea to set anchors in multiple representational systems to create redundancy.

Systemic Interfaces

When you're working with meta-states, you're also working with logical levels and between logical levels. This creates various interfaces between the states which may result in higher frames and states influencing things.

Let's imagine you anchored confidence and you applied it to fear. The result of anchoring as you apply confidence to anger depends on the meaning that "confidence" has to you or another person on a meta-level.

This creates a wide range of semantic constructions that includes, but is not limited to, the following:

- I'm confident I'll overcome my fears.
- I'm confident I'll always be a fearful person.
- I'm confident I'll only get fearful when necessary.

The above example illustrates the importance of the roles higher frames play in meta-stating. Merely accessing confidence and applying it to another state doesn't guarantee anything. It is the person's interpretation of confidence at a higher level that determines everything.

The interface between the levels could also have the effect of reducing the neurological buildup of tension as it does in collapsing of anchors.

Sometimes, attempting to anchor meta-states kinesthetically can backfire and you disperse the neurological energy of the state.

Integral Coalescing

Since meta-states contain an interactive structure involving several layers of states and sometimes states-within-states, it is an ongoing challenge to create coherent integration. Without coherence, you could have all the right variables and still not have the consistency required to cohere as a single unit. This is important if you want a meta-state to last over time.

Coherent integration is completely separate from applying a state to another state, which is something we do all the time. All it takes is asking a meta-question like "would being more appreciative about life, yourself, and others be valuable to you?" This meta-question creates the meta-state of valuing appreciativeness.

The goal of linking states is to do so in a way where they become almost inseparable from one another. The key to achieving this is through repetition and intensity to coalesce the states into a new gestalt or "whole".

Some people who are devoted to self-development may create a meta-state called joyful learning. Eventually, the joy of learning coalesces into the experience of learning so that the person can no longer imagine learning as apart from joy.

The coalescing of meta-states plays a critical role when it comes to working with higher levels and setting multiple frames. Once installed as frames-of-reference and anchored as our felt reality, meta-states become very stable phenomena.

By abstracting and going meta to higher levels, we create the conceptual and presuppositional reality which make up our unconscious frame-of-reference. This creates the reality structure we believe in, those we simply take for granted as "real".

Hall calls this reality structure "the mental and emotional atmosphere by which we live and breathe and have our being."

As we create higher frames by thinking and abstracting, this develops our executive states that we commonly refer to by different meta-terms like understandings, beliefs, values, morals, etc.

Meta-level framing

The process of repetition causes us to store our learning history and references for understanding as higher-level frames. As repetition continues to streamline these frames, they become increasingly outside of awareness. As we lose awareness of these frames, it reinforces them as "reality" leading us to assume that things are the way they are.

CHAPTER 8: META-STATES

At the heart of this process is the meta-state of believing in your beliefs.

Believing in your beliefs creates fanaticism. You can end up boxing yourself into your own model of the world to the extent that you never question it. You go from "I believe" to "I know". You start to become out of touch with your reality and change becomes your greatest foe.

Higher meta-frames can be the reason why you're unable to set empowering meta-states using models and technologies like NLP. There may be a higher frame of reference that eliminates, nullifies, or discounts the empowering meta-state.

Reflexivity

The dominant and determining factor in Meta-States is the self-reflexive consciousness. When we think about our thinking, feel about our feeling, evaluate your evaluations, etc. we transcend the current level of thinking-and-feeling which builds our conceptual frames. The resulting system is our neuro-linguistic and neuro-semantic system of meaning.

Linguistic

Meta-states is a phenomenon which is linguistically formed and drives and requires complex symbols, representations, and meanings. This contrasts with our primary states which are representationally driven via our sights, sounds, sensations, etc.

Anchoring a meta-state requires linking each of the conceptual layers of thoughts and feelings with the necessary words and symbols to encode the embedded framing. This requires symbols sufficient to link the syntax of the embedded layers of these states that are more symbolic or conceptual.

To do this, you can use images, sounds or touches at the meta-level to symbolically stand for the required concept. The sight, sound, or image will not be used literally, but symbolically. You will connect an anchor to these embedded layers as a symbol of the belief, understanding, value, etc.

Since Meta-states takes us into the abstract level of language, words, and other symbolic systems, words will be pre-dominant in this domain as the meta-representational system. Language, as a mental-neurological phenomenon, allows you to stabilize meta-states and sustain them over time to maintain them as enduring phenomena. This is why it's important to choose the right words or symbols to effectively anchor a meta-state.

Higher-level abstractions of language is what allows us to maintain, sustain, and stabilize executive states. Conceptual experiences like beliefs, evaluations, judgments, etc. i.e. meta-states, involve abstract understandings which require language. We can sometimes do this with simple words but it usually requires sentences involving more complex linguistic structures.

If we were to use the meta-state self-esteem as an example, we can see that it requires several layers of complex language such as the following:

- My worth as a person is unconditional.
- Conceptually, my worth as a human being is a given.

- I am somebody simply because I am a human being.

To encode these conceptual understandings, language is required. It's impossible to think about these concepts without words.

It's possible to encode your conceptions into a single image, but first, words are required.

We can take apart words of a negative meta-state which can be disempowering and limiting using the Meta Model. The Meta Model uses a set of questions for exploring and challenging ill-formed semantic structures.

Functionally speaking, the Meta Model questions send you or the person back to the sensory experience from which the toxic map was made and gives you a chance to remap. It allows you to create new and better meta-states that utilize more empowering abstractions from the same sensory-based data.

Unconscious

Meta-states describe your unconscious mind. The unconscious or "subconscious mind" is another systemic property that emerges from meta-states.

Above and beyond almost every state, belief, idea, understanding, etc. are the presence of higher frames that reference and set frames about it. They are typically outside of conscious awareness.

If you want to learn more about your unconscious frames, ask yourself questions about the kind and quality of your states.

An example would be "What is the quality of X?" X represents any state whether it's anger, sadness, happiness, excitement, etc. Adjective and adverbs tell you about your higher meta-states.

* * *

The Meta-Stating Process

The process of creating a new meta-state can be broken up into 7 steps.

Step 1: Awareness

The first step of the meta-stating process is to be consciously aware of where you are, where you want to be, and decide your desired higher-level state.

Step aside yourself for just one moment and embrace a present state awareness of picking your "magic". "Magic" is what Gregory Bateson calls the neurological processes that involve your internal pscyhologics. Since believing, expecting, valuing, etc. can sometimes call something into being, meta-states can seem magical at times.

Here are some questions to ask yourself to help you choose your "magic":

- What higher level mental-emotional state would you like to develop? Resilience? Self-Esteem? Courage?
- What frames of reference would you like to establish in your life? E.g. I either win or learn
- What attitude would you like to build to use as your perceptual filter moving forward? E.g. Everything happens for me, not to me.

As you ask and answer these questions you are meta-stating awareness and perspective.

As mentioned previously in the chapter on NLP Modeling, there are 4 main perceptual positions by which we can gather information: first, second, third, and fourth.

When we are in first perceptual position, we are seeing, feeling, and hearing things from our own perspective. We have no awareness of our higher frames of mind.

By taking a step back and noticing our thinking, feeling, and hearing, we've gone up a meta-level.

When we step aside and look at things from the point-of-view of another person, this is second position, also another meta-state.

In third position, you take another step back and include data from the first 2 positions, and in fourth position, we include the overall system in which both parties operate, which further enriches your perceptual world.

Perceptual positions helps us develop an observational or witnessing meta-state. Korzybski called this the "central mechanism for sanity", the consciousness of abstracting. You're able to witness your own processes and make choices about how to take charge of your mind and state. This helps to increase your sense of choice and control.

Step aside from the space you have been thinking and emoting to a new conceptual space and ask yourself the following questions:

- How would you like to feel?
- How would you like to think?
- How would you like to respond?
- What higher state of mind would you like to entertain about a given situation?

These meta-questions will help you imagine new and better response patterns that will greatly enrich your life.

Step 2: Access

At this point, you're now ready to access a state to apply to your primary state. You can either elicit a state through memory or imagination.

These 2 methods gave rise to the classic NLP elicitations:

- Think about a time when you felt....excited, happy, confident, etc.
- Have you ever experienced....anger, sadness, frustration, etc.
- Have you ever known someone who could X and would be a good model?

- What would it be like..... feel like, look like, sound like, if you stepped into a state of pleasure, gratitude,
- If you imagine being the person who is able to do this, and you step into his or her skin, what is that like?

Whether we use imagination or memory, we're using our thoughts in the form of sensory-based representations, to construct an internal world of VAK (Visual, Auditory, Kinesthetic) as either snapshots or movies.

In order to access a state, you need to use stimuli that has enough intensity so that it evokes you to experience and feel the reference experiences. Elicitation power lies in vividness, intensity, strength of image, sound, feelings, etc. The more drama you bring to your internal world as you represent, the more strength and power you give your elicitations.

Start by accessing the state or meta-state with your cognitive powers. This includes, but is not limited to mind-emotion, imagination, conscience, evaluation, etc. Vividly imagine the state down to the finest details, and make it graphically compelling, then amplify it.

Once you have a clear and compelling image, step into it completely with honest acceptance of it.

In accessing one state to apply to another state, you use the same elements that you would use at the primary level i.e. human thought-and-feelings and physiology. These are the mechanisms that drive mind-body states.

To experience any state, you simply need to access the thoughts of the state fully and completely, step into it with energy and zest, and experience it. You can do it for no reason or for many good reasons. When you know how to use your neuro-linguistic mechanisms, you have a lot of freedom at your fingertips.

Some Meta-States may not involve one single level of states-about-states, but several levels of states-within-states.

When dealing with complex states, you have numerous features to deal with such as the following:

- Primary states
- States linked together through various kinds of anchors
- Emergent gestalts
- Coalesced meta-states
- Feedback and feed-forward loops
- etc.

Step 3: Amplify

When it comes to applying one state to another, you need a certain amount of neurological energy in the state that you put in a meta-position to the first state. If the biological, emotional, and personal energy of the state is relatively low, then you will probably not have enough energy to set the state as a meta-state or a frame over the first state.

As stated previously in "Crash Course on States", States are energy fields. They are also mind-body experiences. We need "enough" of a state in order to set it as a frame. If we don't have sufficient energy, then the result will be inadequate. We will not fully experience the higher frame as a meta-state.

In order to "juice up" a state, we can turn up the cinematic features through the sub-modalities of our internal representations. We can make the colors brighter, the sounds louder, the feelings stronger, etc. We can also hear more compelling words so that as we step into the movie within our minds, we are fully there.

Step 4: Apply

At this point, you're ready to apply one state to the other and link them to each other. There are several ways you can go about linking one state to another.

You can link states by asking a question about the relationship such as:

- What is like when you experience X when you are Y-ing? (E.g. What is it like when you experience motivation when you are learning?)
- How does X transform Y? (E.g. How does respect for other people transform your experience for expressing anger?)

You can also link states through anchoring. Once you anchor the desire of X, you can link that feeling to the target state of Y.

When you're working with a client, you could say something like "Notice what happens when you feel this (fire off anchor) when you are in Y state."

You can also link a state in trance by creating a trance into the new state.

Because higher-level symbols and linguistics drive meta-states, finding and creating empowering words as language inductions enable the state to cohere.

This describes an empowering use of hypnotic language patterns. When we move up logical levels, we go into a trance state and that creates a hypnotic state. The language is hypnotic because the referents are inside of your mind, not in the outside world. To make the sense of the language, you have to go within via downtime hence the origin of the term trance.

Meta-stating uses hypnotic language patterns because it is a hypnotic phenomena. The structure of a meta-state is an induction—a hypnotic induction that builds up and constructs meanings and states.

Richard Bandler and John Grinder said that hypnosis is about using vague language precisely, or being vaguely precise. When we apply one state to another we precisely use vague language to elicit and structure higher-level states. Language induces states and states coalesce through the use of language. This is why memorable, vivid, graphic, and compelling language glues our meta-states and creates a hypnotic induction.

Meta-State inductions tend to take more time, more repetition and more honing to get right because of everything that goes into them. This is also why linguistic anchoring as a form of hypnotic anchoring involves finding just the right words that fit one's values, visions, principles, beliefs, etc.

If you have more than one state to apply to set as a frame, you'll be applying the states in a sequence. Sometimes, the sequence itself is vitally important.

Step 5: Appropriate

In this step, you appropriate the results from your meta-stating to the context and primary state. You appropriate the resources so that the meta-state gestalt comes together.

To do this, step in and fully experience the state. Imagine the state in all its glory and commission your brain and neurology to try it out. As you access these states, appropriate them into the contexts where you want to express the particular meta-state.

Remind yourself that you have immediate access to states anytime you need them. What stop us from appropriating is the limiting belief is that we can't just step in and have these states.

Step 6: Analyze

Check out the meta-state and inspect the values, benefits, congruence, etc. of the appropriated meta-state. Run a quality control of the results of meta-stating your primary state. It may be necessary to step back from the state itself to evaluate it.

A witnessing meta-state can give you enough internal distance to run a quality check on the ecology of your thinking patterns, response patterns, and emotional patterns.

Consider framing your viewpoint from multiple perspectives whether it's friends, family, mentors, etc.

Ask yourself these questions to quality control the meta-state:

- Is this ecological for my life, relationships, health, career, etc.?
- Will this meta-state create any limitations for me?
- Will it empower me to take effective actions as I live my life?
- Will it remain productive for me in the long run?

Remember your states are just experiences of thoughts-and-emotions and sometimes they don't serve you well or enhance your quality of life. In order for a meta-state to be truly empowering, it must not have any significant conflicting states or levels within it.

If you want your meta-states to structure your thinking and feeling in a holistic way, then you will need to integrate all of the layers of your consciousness. Sometimes this means eliminating built-in conflicts between levels and parts. One of the best ways to deal with incongruencies is to meta-model them.

Step 7: Accelerate

It is time to take the new meta-state and accelerate your life and effectiveness. Now is the time to live the new meta-state.

You build a configuration where all of the resources operate as a whole so you can use a coherent structure like a story, narrative, metaphor, etc. The language will glue the strategy together into a single unit and help us experience it as a meaningful whole.

Storytelling and narrative are especially good at organizing meta-experiences. The structure of narrative provides a sequencing that induces, rehearses, and creates various meta-states.

Chapter 9: The Matrix Model

Matrix 101

Ever have that feeling where you're not sure if you're awake or dreaming?
 - Neo, from The Matrix

What is the Matrix? In a way, it's everything and nothing. It operates in the background, and you can't really tell if it's there or not. Our lives are governed by a matrix of beliefs, understandings, and decisions and they operate as a self-organizing system.

Sometimes, our Matrix needs updating. This can be due to negative or unresourceful beliefs or frames. The first step to changing your Matrix is to become aware that it exists and how it operates in your life. Changing matrices becomes a lot simpler once we realize that they're made out of "human stuff". "Human stuff" includes things like thoughts, emotions, and physiology.

Our frames which make up our Matrix is a double-edged sword. They can either empower us or dis-empower us. Out of the potentially hundreds of frames that we have, there are only a handful which are considered essential and define, shape, and govern our lives. Those frames are Self, Power, Others, Time and the World (the 5 sub-matrices of the self) along with State, Meaning and Intentionality.

Our frames encode the meaning we create and hold in mind as the "maps" we use to navigate the experiences of life. Changing a frame, changes the map, which in turn changes the trip. This is best summed up in the basic matrix principle which states "When frames change, so do your life and destiny."

When dealing with a problem, remember that the problem is never you or the other person, it's always the frame. Our frames are just a set of meanings and we can change those meanings if they don't serve us well.

All of us was born into a Matrix. We don't usually call it that. Instead, it goes by different names like mind, personality, self-consciousness, culture, etc. The Matrix was formed over thousands of years. It is made up of layers like belief frames, value frames, understanding and knowledge frames, and religious frames. These frames offer a set of filters, constraints, and maps about self, others, and life. Your Matrix is your internal model of the world and how you use to get around and navigate work and career, relationships, managing yourself and countless other experiences in life.

Unlike other animals, we have the ability to construct meaning. Meaning isn't something we're born with, we have to create it. It's by constructing meaning that we construct the matrices that we live in.

The State Matrix lies at the foundation of all other matrices. This includes everyday states of consciousness. A state is a simple mind-body experience. We all experience mental-emotional and physical states better known as emotions, mood, feelings, attitude, our way of being and personality. We take our states everywhere we go and we're always in some kind of state of mind, state of emotion, and state of body.

Our states have a pervasive influence on our entire beings. They govern our perception, communication, behavior, memory, and learning. We see and perceive the world through the lens provided by our state. States serve a functional purpose in the sense that if we weren't grounded in a state, we would lose our sense of reality as well as our ability to effectively adjust to the world as we find it.

Each of us has a mental movie that plays in our head. Our mental movie is what creates our states. In addition, each matrix in-forms and influences the cinema in our head within the primary experience. Our mental cinema is where we represent things to ourselves over and over again. It is what we sense when we make pictures, hear sounds, and feel sensations as we represent to ourselves prior events and experiences.

States can occur at many levels. When states rise to a higher level, we end up having states about our states or meta-states. Higher states are able to habituate which enables us to keep them. Higher level states stay with you as a frame of mind (like love, joy, stress, etc.) and establishes context for your meanings.

We can't see someone's state when we first encounter them. By learning how to recognize the meanings and frames of one's internal world, we are able to see the invisible matrices of their mind. When we know what movies play in someone's mind-body-emotion matrix, we can get an idea of what that person is feeling and how they'll behave.

Beyond the mental movie are our frames which influence the movie. In other words, we never just think, we think about our thinking. Thinking about our thinking describes our higher levels of mind i.e. operational meta-states. Meta-States allows us to think beyond mere representations. We can also think in terms of editing the mental movie and the camera shots we use.

Our states are influenced by the meaning we assign to things. Our meanings drives and create the layered nature of consciousness. When an external event occurs, we frame things, and when we do that, it activates our state which in turn evoke feelings and behaviors. Humans make meanings at many levels of our mind-body. We create meanings through associating, labeling, defining, languaging, classifying, framing, and evaluating. Each of these terms describe different facets of the same thing which is abstracting or summarizing from one level to another through the use of symbols.

At the primary level, we make association between things i.e. we link our mental-emotional states to our experiences of the world. From there, we make a meta-move to label, classify, frame, language, and evaluate the experience.

We crate all of our other matrices through meaning-making. What you hold in mind becomes your meaning precisely because you hold it mind and use it as your reference structure. We hold our meanings in mind mostly through language. This is partly why the language in NLP was referred to as "the structure of magic" in the 2 original NLP books by that title. The term magic is used because the working of our internal world can almost seem like "magic".

In our internal world, we can make something out of nothing by naming it. For example, you can call generosity into existence simply by labeling some behavior as generous. When we frame something with a particular evaluation to us, it becomes "real" to us. In the inside world of the Matrix, unlike the outside world, naming and speaking it makes it so. It constructs your inner world for what's real to you. Prior to NLP, these processes were known as self-fulfilling prophecies or the placebo effect.

While there are technically 8 sub-matrices that define our Neuro-Semantic System, L. Michael Hall, the creator of the Matrix Model, decided not to number the State Matrix, since it serves as the grounding Matrix. He also admits that 7 is a sexier number than 8, which is hard to argue with.

Each and every matrix attracts and organizes itself according to the meanings incorporated into its frames. One of the higher frame's main function is to attract and command the Matrix to self-organize, making the Matrix dynamic, forever active, and always seeking to make real in the external world what's real on the inside. The highest level frame within any Matrix will determine the focus, motivation and agenda for the default choices you make.

Your awareness and experience of things depend on the movies that play in your mind. Each movie that plays in your mind is informed and framed by each of your sub-matrices. These frames inform and edit your internal mental movies. In Neuro-Semantics, sub-modalities are recognized as the meta-frames that govern the movie itself. They work semantically to encode meaning in sensory-based terms.

Our frames and meta-frames have a way of making sense to us on the inside. This is true even if they're not useful, productive, or logical. Each person lives in a unique universe of perceptions, values, and understandings. Our psycho-logics (as Korzybski would put it) can be incredibly right while also be irrational, painful, ugly, etc. We set the frames by which we invent our own unique "logic" of states within states.

This is why it's important to run ecology checks, reality checks, and quality control checks on your frames. That's the only way you can test the usefulness, productivity, and sanity of your Matrix. We cannot do so from the inside of the psycho-logical structure.

You can see someone's Matrix by paying attention to their language patterns and nonverbal responses. As matrices get activated, you can recognize them in a person's neurology and physiology. When a person goes into a state, you can hear it in their language that activates a given matrix. A person's matrix is also activated when their internal semantics are activated regarding some meaning that the person considers important.

Let's say you have a person who's a very religious Christian and they hear someone cursing Jesus' name. Because their religion plays a strong role in their life and makes up a significant part of their Matrix, it's likely their Matrix will get activated and could include a wide range of responses from anger, fear, disgust, or even indifference.

Hall recommends thinking of the Matrix as a hologram and imagine the different matrices flashing on and off as they are activated by information entering the system and energy leaving the system. This brings us to our next point which is that there are multiple feedback and feed-forward loops in our Neuro-Semantic system. These describe the information being brought in and processed and the energy being created and manifested in the world.

The first feedback loop occurs at the primary state level in the input-output or stimulus-response process. The world "out there" impacts upon you some inciting incident and you respond. Information comes in as feedback. Then you expand energy which goes out as you feed-forward behavior and emotion. That is the horizontal loop.

The second feedback loop is a vertical loop, which is the meta-state loop of meaning-making. In this case, you feed information back to yourself as you think and send it upwards to higher levels of mind. From there, you can then feed that information forward in your bodies. This activates your body in terms of neurology and physiology so that you begin to embody the information into muscle memory and response pattern. This results in emotions, speech, and behavior which you then feed-forward into your world.

The 7 matrices are always ready to be activated by current conditions and stimuli. They are always in the back of your mind i.e. outside of conscious awareness, and make up much of what you would call your "unconscious" mind. If your frames are well-formed and robust, they will empower you to be automatically effective and intuitive about the right things to do. On the other hand, if they're ill-formed and fragile, then they will greatly limit you and create self-sabotage and dis-ease throughout your whole system. You will feel like "reality is your enemy" and that you're in the wrong. This is a sign that something is wrong with your matrix world. It's not you that's wrong, it's your frames.

CHAPTER 9: THE MATRIX MODEL

Matrix Analysis is the process that allows you to understand the neuro-semantic system as a system. It allows you to identify the driving and critical matrix within and behind every experience. Through Matrix Analysis, you're able to profile groups, cultures, yourself, etc. and to understand the structure of an experience. In this way, you can use the matrix for modeling any experience, emotion or skill.

Hall also recommends thinking of the Matrix as a holoarchy (similar to Meta-States) rather than a hierarchy. A holoarchy is comprised of holons, which are both a part and a whole. The whole is in the part and the part is in the whole. When you think of your states like holons, you can understand your mind-body-emotion system as a system. By thinking of your mind-body system as a holoarchy, you can take any word, belief, cinematic feature of the movie, etc and by playing with it, you can flush out the whole that's within it i.e. the higher frames that govern the neuro-semantic system.

According to Neuro-Semantics, our mind-body-and-emotion experience works as a system. It operates as a total system of frames which are embedded in higher frames. All of these frames work as a system of interactive parts mutually influencing one another.

The Matrix Model unites all of the component pieces, distinctions, patterns and models of NLP. Additionally, it provides a framework for how to use NLP effectively as a coach, manager, leader, therapist or communicator. It also integrates the 4 Meta-Domains of NLP, the 4 higher domains which govern key facets of human functioning:

- Language (The Meta Model)
- Perception and Thinking Patterns (Meta-Programs)

- The Levels of State (Meta-States)
- The Cinematic Features of our Representations ("Sub-modalities")

Finally, the matrix unifies within one structure the meta-stating processes which include all of the systemic processes involved in meaning-making layers.

In Hall's book, The Matrix Model, he states that he uses the word matrix in 2 different ways: one as a mathematical term and the other in reference to the movie "The Matrix". A matrix with 2 or 3 axises can be used to create new concepts and understandings. For example, if we relate the ideas of speed and time, we can construct miles per hour.

When we apply the term "matrix" to human psychology and functioning, it refers to all of the frames of mind we hold. These frames include belief frames, value frames, reference frames, and so on. There are also frames within embedded frames which make up systems of understanding.

All of us live in a matrix of our creation. We do not deal with the world directly but our model of the world i.e. our mental maps. We relate to the world via 3 mapping levels: neurological mapping, representation mapping, and conceptual mapping. This is similar, yet different from the 3 semantic levels we covered earlier in the section on NLP Presuppositions.

Neurological maps is the first level in which we relate to the world. You experience things at this level as perceptions. Your perceptions emerge from the interaction of your sensory receptors with the energy manifestations "out there". Because our perceptions seem so real to us, we can easily confuse what we "see" with what is truly out there. Our perceptions are constructed in our body and brain in the interaction of the external energies impacting our neurology.

Representational mapping is the next level after neurological. At this level, we go within and recall and represent sights, sounds, sensations, and smells of your experience in the theater of your mind. You then use various cinematic features of these sensory systems i.e. your sub-modalities to encode your internal cinema. You can code your movies in color or black-and-white. You can make it blurry in focus. You can zoom in or out, and so on. All of this creates your "movie mind", how you represent things.

Lastly, we relate to the world via our conceptual maps. By drawing conclusions, generalizing, and computing what things mean, you construct concepts, categories, beliefs, values, decisions, etc. You can then bring these abstract frames to your thinking and use them as categories of understanding.

All of these frames of reference come together to create your Matrix. They comprise your reality strategy and give you your sense of the fabric of reality. Your matrix has you to the extent that you're not aware of the existence of your subjective world of frames.

Your Matrix pulls a conceptual wool over your eyes so that you stop seeing, hearing, and feeling at sensory levels. To see things fresh and from a beginner's mindset, you have to "lose your mind and come back to your senses" as Fritz Perls would put it. When you take the red pill, like Neo did in the matrix, you open your eyes and ears and feeling to the map/territory difference and you begin to discover the depth and length of the rabbit holes you've created in your mind.

You can have a choice about which Matrix you live in by first knowing about the Matrix and developing skills for entering and exiting the Matrix. All of the games that you play in life spring from the higher frames that are set in your mind. The first skill you need to develop to become a Matrix Master is Matrix Awareness. You must become aware of your own Matrix and get a sense of your Matrix and how it plays out in your life.

Hall says "Matrix awareness begins as you come to understand how you re-present see-hear-feel information to yourself in your mental movies and then create mental maps of those representations as you classify, frame, and meta-state those understandings. Frame awareness, and how frames are embedded inside of yet other frames, describes how you inevitably and naturally meta-state yourself and use your self-reflexive consciousness to create layers of embedded frames."

Consider thinking of your Matrix as an operating system for how you make or create meaning which then generates your model of the world. We can see how the 4 Meta-Domains of NLP come together in the meaning-making funnel:

- The Meta Model describes the linguistic structuring of meaning.
- Meta-States describe the framing levels of states and meaning which you layer level upon level.
- Meta-Programs, as solidified Meta-States, describe the frames that become the perceptual filters and thinking patterns and coalesced into your muscle memory.
- Meta-Modalities ("sub-modalities") describe representational meaning that show up as the cinematic features in your internal

movies.

Framing and Re-framing requires us to "go meta". When you move to a meta-position, you are able to step aside from your first thinking and feeling and to think-and-feel about it which creates the next level. This allows us to set new frames, categories, classifications, and meanings.

The Matrix is experienced in states. Therefore, understanding and managing your states is essential for matrix awareness. A matrix system cannot be activated unless you're in the right state. We usually shift from one state to another fairly easily. We constantly shift states throughout the day.

However, there are some states that stay for the long haul. This can happen with an especially strong state. By increasing the intensity of the state, it not only affects your surface-level thinking but it also affects your deepest or highest state of mind and emotion. This is known as state-dependency. Sometimes these states can reverberate throughout your system not only for hours but days.

We can also make states stay by meta-stating and setting one state solidly in your mind-body-emotion system such that it becomes your frame of mind. When this happens, the state becomes the way you think-and-feel about something. We call these states "attitudes" because they seem so solid and stable. They can last years or decades.

When you Meta-State yourself or others, the Matrix emerges. You create layer upon layer of concepts which create the labyrinth of your mind. When you meta-state frames of mind and meanings that stay, you create your own essential Matrix which is made up of 7 sub-matrices. These 7 are so fundamental to being human that you carry them with you wherever you go. They are based upon and centered around, your primary states.

* * *

Matrix 102

In order to enter someone's Matrix, you need to be able to build rapport, have a sense of safety, and a certain amount of respect for the other person's Matrix. Building rapport should be nothing new for a NLPer, and respecting the other person's matrix is the same as respecting the other person's model of the world, because that is what the matrix essentially is. You can't even access your own Matrix if you treat yourself disrespectfully, let alone, someone else's.

As L. Michael Hall puts it "Judgment locks the doors of the Matrix". If you judge yourself or other people, then you won't be able to enter the matrix of frames. The key to entering someone's Matrix is acceptance.

When you say hello to someone, you're going to get a certain response. The response you get gives you the first bit of information about that person's frames. Responses only make sense relative to the frame it emerged from. All matrices are invisible until they're activated. Matrices get activated by information and activity, which are the same things that transform the matrix. The deeper you go into someone's Matrix, the more information you receive and the more frames you activate.

Matrices spin and spiral as a person goes round and round this neuro-semantic system to make sense of their experiences. Matrices can spiral out of control if we create a negative downspiral of thoughts and feelings which causes to feel worse and worse. On the other hand, matrices can spiral upward and create virtuous thoughts and emotions around something that fills you with joy and happiness. Generally, our matrix will spiral as a balancing system which helps bring us to a state of equilibrium. This is the self-organizing and self-fulfilling nature of our matrix of frames.

You can enter someone's matrix by matching-and-mirroring what they say or do. By doing this, you pace the person's reality and validates it so that the person feels heard and understood. This allows them to feel safe in your presence. You can enter your own matrix through acceptance and appreciation and respectfully welcome your frames as frames (remember the map isn't the territory) and seek first to understand. This means hearing and seeing your reality for what it is rather than what you want it to be.

Everyone has their own unique matrix. No one lives in the same universe as you do. You can tell you're in the presence of a different Matrix when you say things like:

- I can't get inside his head.
- I have no idea where they're coming from.
- I can't relate to this person at all.

It's normal to come across matrices different from ours. That's bound to happen. What causes problems is the attitude towards the difference. Ideally, you should try to understand how their matrix differs, why it differs, what a particular matrix seeks to do that's of value, and how it came to be constructed as a solution to a perceived problem.

Every time we create a "map" about something, we create more frames. Our matrix grows from how we take the experiences of life and map our understandings and beliefs. Each content matrix is a matrix of belief frames about a given domain of experience and concept: self, power, others, time, and world. Our beliefs frames embedded in higher frames, coded linguistically, comprise our model of the world.

Each person's Matrix contains the best knowledge and understanding that the person has at that moment. With that in mind, when it comes to dealing with other people's matrices, start by assuming it makes sense. It may not make sense to you, at least not at first, but it makes sense to the person who mapped things that way. Once you assume it makes sense, you can explore how it makes sense to that person.

L. Michael Hall argues that the most important Matrix is the Meaning Matrix. This is because it involves the person's meaning-making skills, which includes classifying, defining, languaging, framing, associating, and evaluating, by which the person creates all of the other Matrices. You build your Matrix as you create meaning and you hold those meanings in your mind-body-emotion system. We use the term "meaning" as the ideas which you hold in your mind and from which you build your other ideas.

All embedded frames within frames are meta-states. The Meaning Matrix is also referred to as a meta-stating funnel. As you move up the levels, these "logical levels" of the mind contain multi-dimensional perspectives that we commonly refer to as values, beliefs, understandings, etc. These are abstract concepts which become stable through language and repetition. These terms don't refer to different things but different ways of looking at the same thing.

Your Matrix can be grounded or ungrounded. Grounded means that your Matrix is connected to your everyday life. In order to ground your Matrix, you connect it to sensory-based referents such as things you either see, hear, feel, etc. When matrices aren't grounded, they tend to spiral out of control and have little to no connection with the real world. Since we don't deal with the world directly, but our maps (i.e. matrix), it's possible to become ungrounded. When this happens, you generally feel off-center and unable to move forward.

When working with someone else's Matrix, Halls recommends the following dictum: "Follow the person's energy as it moves through the Matrix." This refers to recognizing how information enters into and flows through the person's mind-body system as it energizes and activates the system. This is a highly advanced skill and beyond the scope of this book. However, this tracking is essential for modeling human experiences. By doing this, you can track the representational steps as they flow through the system.

Matrix activation enables you to see the sub-matrices turn on and off as information travels through your neuro-semantic system. What was once invisible becomes visible as you activate it through information and symbolic input. Halls like to imagine the Matrices flickering on and off like lights and energy fields as different energies move through it.

You can listen for the "heart" of the matrix and try to figure out what the Matrix cares most about. Notice what the Matrix is built around. Is it positive or negative? Empowering or limiting? Enriching or toxic? You can think of the "heart" of the matrix as attractions and aversions that create your drive and energy.

Meta-frames filter and select both what we see and how you see the world. This description of meta-frames defines what is known as the NLP Model of "Meta-Programs". Meta-Programs refers to those programs that operate at a level above (or meta) to the content of our thoughts. What you talk about is the content, structure refers to how you are talking and the frames of reference you use in your talking. As the second meta-domain of NLP, Meta-Programs offer an additional tool for modeling the structure of experience. As meta-level processes, Meta-Programs function as an operating system for processing information and thinking. Because of this, they reflect a person's thinking pattern and style.

Hall states "A person's mental focus as his perceptual lenses describes the way he conceptually sees the world. By recognizing Meta-Programs as an important aspect of his Matrix, what we call Meta-Programs are structural aspects of the Matrix." In other words, your matrix of frames is in one sense, your perceptual lenses. They are similar but different.

According to Dr. Pascal Gambardella, a person who's researched extensively the relationship between Meta-Programs and the Matrix Model came up with this working definition: X is a Meta-Program if X filters what we perceive or what we attend to.

Hall posits that Meta-Programs arise as integrated Meta-States. They emerge from meta-states which coalesce to become part of your neurology and encoded into muscle memory. Meta-States creates the foundation of Meta-Programs. Meta-Programs result from meta-stating one thought or feeling with another. This makes Meta-Programs integrated and solidified meta-states. We can therefore conclude that every Meta-Program started off as a meta-state.

Our perceiving patterns start off as mind-body states made up of particular thoughts, emotions, and physiologies. By using them consistently, they become habitual. Eventually, you use it reflectively in all of your thinking. It becomes your perceptual pattern, or Meta-Program.

Every state involves a particular way of seeing things. In anger, you see the world in terms of threats and dangers and feel aggressive. We have a much different perception of the world when we're feeling calm or at peace. In every perception, we're in some of kind of mind-body-emotion state.

Through the various NLP meta-models, we have 4 different ways to describe things:

- Focusing on the state and level of mind - Meta-State
- Focusing on perception and way of seeing things - Meta-Programs
- Focusing on language and way of talking - Meta-Model
- Focusing on the representation which are edited and coded into a person's mental movie - we call them cinematic features i.e. sub-modalities.

We have 4 different systems or models for describing the same thing: the structure our subjective experience. Each model provides a different facet of the same thing and enriches our understanding.

Meta-Programs can also arise when someone brings value to a state. For example, if you believe in the importance of being punctual, you outframe the first state (being punctual) with value and significance. There are a multitude of ways we can construct a meta-program using various state structures. Examples include fearful about being late, joyful about being on time, disgust for people who are late, etc.

Repeating any meta-state leads to creating a habituating pattern we can call either a meta-state or meta-program. Sometimes, these meta-structures become a new category called a Gestalt State. Gestalt states has are described in early Meta-States books by Hall as a "canopy of consciousness". He uses this phrase to illustrate the fact that specific Meta-States can so completely "engulf" another state that it creates, in a sense, an entire mental atmosphere or context. When a person's canopy of consciousness becomes the very fabric of their emotional and mental life, it becomes what we call the Matrix.

Meta-Programs arise from Meta-States, and the more you value, believe in, and appreciate the meta-state, the more you create a driver meta-program. A driver meta-programs means that the state and its programs ("set of operational frames") for how you perceive, sort and process information becomes your default operating style. It is your "way of being" in the world.

In a driver meta-program, your primary states are embedded inside of a larger context made up of meta-states that form the meta-program. Most NLP Meta-Programs fit into the Meaning Matrix because they relate to how we think and how we create meaning in the first place. Meta-Programs enable you to identify the matrix of frames upward into a person's labyrinth of frames.

* * *

Grounding Matrix

States Matrix

Bearing in mind that the Matrix is the neuro-semantic system of embedded frames within frames, it would make sense that it shows up in our state. The Matrix is grounded in everyday states of mind, body, emotion. When it comes down to it, our states and meta-states are made out of the "stuff" of mind and body. When we layer our states, emergent properties arise and we create higher states that are more than the sum of their parts. These are known as Gestalt states.

Our higher levels of mind also emerge from our primary states and are expressed in them. As such, we begin and end in state. Since sub-matrices operate in states, they are to a certain extent, state-dependent. If you can change your state sufficiently, your matrix will also change. Sometimes, the entire Matrix changes.

States are mind-body experiences: reflecting your awareness at given point in time. They are made up of 3 components: what's on your mind, your physiology i.e. physical body, and what you're currently feeling, also known as emotions. You can use these 3 components to do a state check by asking yourself the following questions:

- What's on my mind?
- How am I feeling in my body?
- What emotions am I currently experiencing?

States are dynamic, fluid, and always changing. We go through hundreds of state changes in a day. You're always in some state, it's just a matter of what state you're in at any given time. Here are some questions, courtesy of L. Michael Hall, to help you explore your states and develop state awareness:

- What state are you in right now?
- How much control do you have over your state?
- What other states have you experienced today?
- What states would be resourceful that you are missing?

States are made up of mind, body, and emotion. They are made out of the representations and ideas in your mind. In our mental screen, we represent sight, sounds, and sensations that you've experienced. We do this by creating a "mental movie" of events, people, places, etc. While it may seem like we're internally seeing, hearing, and, feeling, in actuality, we're not. But, it is a useful metaphor for thinking about and experiencing your representations and gives you a sense of how you code your "thoughts".

In addition to sensory information, we also use words to define and describe things. Words give us a higher sense of how to make sense out of things. Language operates as a "sixth sense" and is the meta-representation system for the VAK representational systems. Words describe more "stuff" of the mind.

The condition of your body profoundly impacts your states. If you don't believe me, try going without food or sleep for a few days (please don't) and notice how your body feels. You'll quickly learn just how much your body affects your everyday states. Even the way we move, breathe, and gesture can induce particular states. For example, if you slump your shoulders, exhibit shallow breathing, and move timidly, you will find it impossible to be positive and optimistic.

Emotions emerge as the body registers the value and meaning of the mind. We call the result "psycho-somatic". Emotions arise from the body's registering of an evaluation. They mostly derive from your thinking and cognition, however our emotions can also induce certain ways of thinking.

States are activities and processes of the mind-body system as an interaction with the world. We can quickly change our states when we're on the receiving end of lots of life-changing events. We can also change states quickly when we choose to alter our lives.

We generally experience consciousness as a sort of stream where people, events, and circumstances just occur around you. Things flow in and out. State appears to be a thing that happens to us at this level. When a strong trigger occurs, it jars our awareness and dramatically grabs our attention. We may become much more intense and our steady stream of consciousness becomes like a rushing torrent. It might seem like we're in a downward spiral that makes us feel worse and worse.

When we're in the thick of it, the best thing we can do is just let it happen. Fighting against it won't help you. These thoughts that are popping up are coming from the higher levels of the many dimensions of your Matrix.

States have varying degrees of intensity. We normally don't notice a state until it becomes sufficiently strong. If the state is not intense, then it will be just below your conscious awareness. Even though we're always in a state, we may not know what state we're in at any given time. To illustrate, when you're in your comfort zone, it doesn't seem like you're in any particular state. The same is true for habituated thoughts and emotions. Everything will seem so normal and regular that you will not be able to make any clear distinctions.

It's possible to habituate into negative and toxic states and we should avoid doing so for obvious reasons. Negative states can become normal if they become habituated. You could even develop a burning desire for it if you're deprived of it. That's the power of the Matrix.

The intensity of an emotional state is determined by how much you have that state and how much you could get caught up in that state so that the state could "have" you. In Neuro-Semantics, states are gauged for intensity to set a higher meta-state as a frame of mind. This is generally needed to have sufficient neurological intensity when we bring one state to another and create a meta-state. To gauge a state, you can ask a question like "Where are you on a scale from 0 to 10 with your [insert state here]"?

The more emotionally intense a state, the more you will experience state dependency. When this phenomenon occurs, it will seem as if the state has taken on a life of its own. The state will determine and govern your memory, perception, learning, behavior, and thinking. It will seem as if the state has taken over what you see and how you see. It's called state dependency because you become dependent on the state rather than the state be dependent on you - your choices, your thoughts, your beliefs, etc.

States are neither good nor bad. They are just experiences we're having at any given moment in time. States by themselves are amoral. Morality and ethics arise from what you do and how you behave while in a state. It is more beneficial to evaluate states in terms of usefulness, practicality, and resourcefulness.

To do that we can ask quality control questions:

- Is this state enhancing or impoverishing?
- Does this state bring out my best?
- Is this state ecological?

States are the result of countless bits of information, thinking, feeling, and neurology so because of that, states are neutral. Primary states are textured by the higher meta-states of the Matrix. We experience our higher levels of mind as part of our primary consciousness or mind. This happens because meta-states penetrate into the primary state. We cannot get away from the primary states that ground us to a certain time, place, situation, or context. These are the states that ground you in the moment and in your current experience and set the foundation for all of your other thoughts and self-reflexivity about things.

What you experience in the higher levels of mind collects and accumulates into your everyday states. You experience what occurs at your higher levels of your mind and the system as a whole, in your present state of mind and body as feelings. This influences your mental movie in such a way that it frames what you are seeing, hearing, and feeling. It affects how you adjust the lenses of your mental camera. Here we can see the whole is in the part and the part is in the whole.

The present state is the fundamental reference point for understanding any given Matrix. To find out someone's state, you can ask them questions about what state they're in and what triggers it, the nature and quality of the state, the context and environment of the state, etc.

Along with state, the coding and quality of the state is just as important. The mental cinema is important because it is through representations that we "make sense" out of the world. This creates the inside world of your inner reality. We determine what's real to us by the movie playing in our mind. In exploring the structure of experience, ask about the cinema that's playing in one's mind. You can use that as an entry point into one's Matrix:

- What are you representing in the theater of your mind?
- How are you representing it in audio-visual terms?
- What perspective are you taking in reference to this movie?

Many states occur, and can only occur when you're in a particular state or environment. When we're in a different state, a particular Matrix may not be accessible and will not work.

States are driven, not just by our frames but by different facets of our neurology or biology that are more innate. According to William Glasser, we have 5 basic needs for survival: survival, love and belonging, power, freedom, and fun. He refers to these as built-in urges or drives that motivate us. Others have suggested biological needs like sex, oxygen, water, food, etc. Safety and security is another set of needs which include stability, protection, control, etc. Social needs include the need for love and affection, connection, bonding, etc. Self needs include the need for recognition, acknowledgment, validation, etc. Beyond our "animal needs" are our human needs for knowledge, meaning, beauty, humor, etc. All of these and any other innate drive in human nature are part of our primary states.

State Management as we define it is commonly referred to as Emotional Intelligence. This refers to the emotional awareness, emotional monitoring, emotional regulations (self-control), and emotional connecting with others (relating, bonding, etc.). These higher meta-states allow you to choose your states and direct them which is a primary focus of NLP and Neuro-Semantics.

* * *

Meta-States & The Matrix

Meta-stating allows us to texture and qualify any primary or grounding states in a multitude of different ways. By doing this, we make the first state richer and fuller. Texturing a state can either enhance or inhibit a person. On the negative end, you can apply a negative meta-state that's toxic or destructive. On the positive end, a meta-state can empower a person so that they become more skilled, competent, focused or any other desirable quality.

As adults, our states almost never occur alone. This is because as soon as we enter a primary state, we start having thoughts and feelings about that state, and just like that, we make a meta-move to create multiple layers of meta-states. We use higher states to texture our primary states which creates our Matrix.

Reflexivity is what creates the meta-states. You reflect upon yourself via your thoughts, feelings, emotions, experiences, etc. According to Alfred Korzybski, the consciousness of abstraction is the foundation of sanity. This higher level awareness is what allows you to check and re-check your own abstracting, commonly referred to as thinking, representing, computing, reasoning, etc. When you're not conscious of your evaluating or abstracting, you run the risk of jumping logical levels and setting meta-frames without knowing what or how you're doing it.

Hall has a concept called interference which refers to the fact that when you enter, or re-enter, your own system of thoughts-and-feelings by way of reflexive awareness, you interfere with your own thoughts-and-feelings. You interfere in the sense that your second- and third-order thoughts and so on will either conflict or support your primary awareness. The interference can either lead to negative states or "dragon states", a term coined by Hall, or create resourceful states like optimism, courage, resilience, etc.

Symbols are another way we can reflect upon ourselves and create additional layers of frames. Symbols and symbolic systems include things like language, mathematics, music, etc. Both symbol systems and reflexivity are infinite processes. In other words, whatever you say or think about something, you can always add another thought or feeling about that level. Our reflexivity ability allows us to operate at different levels of awareness and abstracting. The hierarchy of ideas mentioned earlier in the book is a practical application of this.

We can think of reflexivity as infinite progress. We can always take "one more step" for whatever we're thinking, feeling, or experiencing. If we ever find ourselves in a position where we're stuck, we can always step forward and create another level and out-frame our experience and create new possibilities.

We can create layers of meaning through framing, evaluating, applying standards, and meta-stating. All meaning-making processes involve taking bits and pieces of thoughts, emotions, memories, etc and applying them to your previous state. In this way, we meta-state up the levels of meaning, abstractions, and classifications. You meta-state the essential matrices of your mind about yourself, what you can and cannot do, time, power, others, the world, and your intentions. When you put all of this together, you have structural form to your meanings. This is how words (inside the nervous system of a human being) become so semantically loaded. If you load up a words with a lot of significance, it can have a powerful effect on one's neurology.

Our internal psycho-logics refers to our internal world. On the inside, everything makes sense to us. This is true even when those beliefs or concepts are toxic, painful, unproductive, etc. We create these internal worlds layer by layer using the best thinking and feeling we had at the time.

If you meta-state yourself with a thought or feeling and it seems important in some way or you experience in an emotionally intense way, it will stay with you as a frame of reference. You meta-state your individual matrices and your overall Matrix into existence. Then you confirm, validate, and make them so. We have numerous terms for describing meta-stating functions like framing, classifying, categorizing, etc. These processes allow us to create layer upon layer of meaning as we set higher contexts as frames about things. These become our contextual frames.

All of us have multiple meta-state structures of frames within frames within frames that influence things. All of these influences show up in our state. To flush out meta-levels encoded and embedded inside a state, ask meta-level questions:

- What is your quality of joy? (or anger, confidence, doubt, etc.)
- What do you believe about x?
- What's your intention in experiencing that state?

Since we can experience emotion at different levels of mind, this means that our primary states and meta-states influence the kind and quality of emotion. Primary state emotions tend to be very direct, immediate, and kinesthetically active. When you experience emotion at the primary level, it's easier to identify the external trigger that set it off and the internal body part wherein you register that emotion.

Meta-state emotions are emotions triggered by concepts, rather than events. They can be experienced just as fully, if not more so, after the event. When you recall and rehearse the event, you can do so while intensifying and amplifying the concept. You'll often experience meta-emotions more in your head than your body. But this isn't always the case. Sometimes, the meta-emotion will become embodied and you'll feel it much more in you body. Also, with repetition, meta-emotions move from mind to muscle and become incorporated in the body.

* * *

Process Matrices

Meaning Matrix

Each person slowly builds their Matrix over the years through their experiences. We do so by mapping various ideas, beliefs, emotions, decisions, etc. about things. Our experiences don't create our matrix, it's the mapping of our experiences via mean-making, conceptualizing, learning, and so on, that creates the Matrix. In other words, your experiences don't comprise the center of your Matrix, your meanings do.

Your ideas are more than your experiences. They're more important in defining yourself and setting the course for the future. The Meaning Matrix is not only the first Matrix, but it's also the most important and critical of the Matrices. The Meaning Matrix begins at the level of state via the State Matrix and spirals all the way up the levels of our neuro-semantic states of mind. We meta-state our way up these levels. Our meaning-making process becomes more complex over time as we make meanings in different ways at different levels of mind and at different times in our development.

The Meaning Matrix is where you create classification meanings. By using categories and definitions, you speak the other matrices into existence as you construct them and make them real to yourself. The words you use and the definitions you create determine to a great extent the realities you experience. Definitions are not neutral. They're semantically loaded. Words can set frames, evoke emotions, and associate you into experiences.

The Meaning Matrix is how we associate things that may or may not be connected normally. Beyond the primary level of meaning, we create frame meanings. These are the meanings that arise as you set frames-of-reference that define the significance of things. In this way, we create multiple layers of embedded frames of meanings within frames. By doing this, we meta-state ourselves more and more into our Matrix. Even after the Meaning Matrix calls all of the other matrices into existence, it continues to operate as you set frames, attach emotions, and create evaluations that influence the whole Matrix.

The Meaning Matrix has a simple 2-step process. First, we use the Meaning Matrix to relate an external event to an emotional state. Then, we use it to classify and categorize things. With each layer of meaning we add, we spiral around in our mind about that meaning, layering even more meanings. The significance and value of the meanings you invent create your internal universe. It is through the creation of meaning that you know what to call things, how to interpret events, and how to perceive the significance of anything. We have to learn how to attribute meaning to things and there is great freedom in the range of meanings we can attribute. The Meta-Model can be used as a description for understanding how you use language to encode those meanings at a linguistic level and how to effectively question those constructs.

We're all born inside of meaning-making matrices called family systems, communities, religions, politics, etc. As we grow, we absorb the style and content from each of those meaning systems. Those systems include the meaning-making results of those who came before us and who left behind symbol systems which encode their meanings. This time-binding mechanism explains why meanings seem to exist outside of us.

Language is the most obvious time-binding symbol. When we externalize language, it encodes the definitions, classifications, and categories of others. There's also written media like books and magazines. On a cultural level, meaning can be made external in rituals, plays, movies, art, etc. Meaning does not exist by itself but can only be transmitted by such things, events, and experiences. They're the symbols of meaning but it takes a meaning-maker to "make sense" of them. If the meaning isn't passed on, the symbol becomes empty.

Here are some questions to help you explore your Meaning Matrix:

- How do you interpret this?

- What does this mean to you?
- If you had the choice of giving it a new meaning, one that would enhance you, what would you invent?

When creating meaning, you create, search for, and explore those things you consider important or value. Our attribution style arises from the Meaning Matrix. This is the style that you use to interpret what things mean. This speaks about the quality and properties of your meaning-making.

Here are some questions to explore your attribution style:

- Do you treat things as they count or you discount things?
- Do you create positive or negative meanings?
- Do you view life as a problem to be solved or as something beautiful to experienced?

You also create representational meaning by your style of editing and coding your mental movies. This has been given the name "sub-modalities", which is a bit of a misnomer. They are better thought of as the finer cinematic details of a person's mental movie. The cinematic features describe how you represent things in the theater of your mind in terms of sight (visuals), sounds (auditory), and sensations (kinesthetic). As sensory information, the features of your movie act similarly to control knobs on a tv set from back in the day. You can turn the brightness up or down, fade the color out or make it more vivid, You can edit the soundtrack with various features like tonality, melody, loudness, etc.

The cinematic features determine how compellingly real you feel your representations or constructs, or how vague or non-compelling. For example, if you encode your cinema with all the features of being present, big, close, 3D, and you are inside of the movie - you will typically install whatever idea you are viewing or whatever belief you are inventing very quickly. Yet, if you observe the movie from the 3rd person, then you will experience it as only informational and not necessarily emotional or motivational. Neuro-Semantics refers to the cinematic features of the movie as "Meta-Modalities".

You use your mind-body-emotions to map your understanding of things that make up the world or territory. According to Korzybski in Science and Sanity, our sensory receptors abstract or summarize the energy manifestations "out there" to create within us neurological maps of the territory. From there, we abstract to the next level to create neurological mappings of neurological mappings i.e. our cognitive unconscious. Eventually, we create a linguistic mapping and then higher linguistic mapping. This is how the nervous-system brain comes to "know" and "understand" things.

Meaning starts off as "sense impressions". From there, our "senses" activate and then begin the levels of neurological mapping. This goes on until our "mental" sense of perception arises in our mental theater. Once it's in our mental theater, we can use linkage, classifying, naming, defining, and so on, over and over again we map things linguistically. This allows us to do multiple layers of reflexive layering of frames. This is what creates the Matrix we live in.

Beliefs don't start as beliefs. First, they're just rudimentary thoughts, ideas, and information that we see-hear-feel. Our beliefs are higher level frames. From our beliefs, we can create even higher levels as we layer frames upon frame to create a whole series of embedded frames. Generally, our thoughts are embedded within various contexts and those contexts are within contexts. This is what's called a matrix of frames within which you give birth to your meanings.

Most things that pass through our mind never stays. We have to actively hold thoughts, beliefs, memories, etc. in our mind in order for them to become our meanings. When you explore meaning in yourself or in someone else, you're exploring what the person holds in their mind about something. When you ask someone, "What do you mean by that?", you want to know both what's on their mind (the mental movie) and what's in the back of their mind i.e. all of the context and frames which sets the stage for understanding and comprehending.

Mental frames govern our actions. The thoughts we carry with us make up our Matrix, the sum of our embedded frames. The higher the thoughts, the more outside of consciousness aware they will be. The higher level intentions and understandings by which you interpret things determine your meanings.

The first level of meaning is our sensory-based movie. The building blocks of our mind is the internal representations of sights, sounds, sensations, smells, and taste. Above this level are the words we use, the meta-representational system. Above this level are even higher levels of abstract language.

Meaning comes from the mind, it doesn't exist outside of us. Our meaning emerges as a neuro-linguistic product that we construct from our interactions with the outside world including people, events, ideas, etc. This internal construct is an interaction of event and thought. We interact with things, events, and ideas and then create representations we hold in our minds.

We are the meaning-makers and we can bring our meanings under control if we want to. External events are only as meaningful as you make them out to be. Meaning is a dynamic process of thinking, feeling, and framing. The more you accept the idea that meaning is always changing, the less likely you'll treat it as something permanent. Since meaning arises from mind and by mind, we can expect it to come and go according to the functioning of our consciousness.

To illustrate how meaning cannot exist from a meaning, consider someone who is about to go to college. That could mean different things depending on your mood, thoughts, and values. Becoming a college student could mean "adopting a whole new identity" or the "start of a new chapter in your life." Or it could feel like a massive burden that you're ill-prepared for.

We tend to project meaning onto the world. This gives the illusion that meaning is something "out there". We also have habitual thoughts and ideas that makes it seem like there's permanence in our meanings when there isn't. We construct all of our internal realities. It is up to us to construct useful maps.

We first create meaning through a process called "linking". We link one thing to another. That is the basis of the stimulus-response mechanism as demonstrated by Pavlov's dog experiment. We call the relationship between external stuff and internal stuff "meaning". In Hall's book titled "Mind-Lines", this relationship is formulated as External Behavior = Internal State or EB = IS for short. This describes the meaning-making process.

As we move through life, we can't help but link things to one another. Sometimes, our linking doesn't create an accurate map of things. Once an idea or experience is linked with something else, the idea will get embodied in our muscles.

Linking things together allows us to construct various ideas about reality. Whatever you say leads to, is equal to, or is the same as something else becomes so to you inside of your neurology. Gregory Bateson and the co-founders of NLP described this as "magic" because it seems like one thing magically becomes something else.

We can model this "magic" using the Meta-Model by borrowing 2 key linguistic distinctions:

- Cause-Effect Statements - X leads to Y. "You're always on your phone because you're texting someone else."
- Complex Equivalence (CEq) X means Y. "Failing your test means you're a loser."

When humans creates meanings, it always occur in frames. We can think and feel our thoughts to virtually no end. This factor is what enables us to build layers of meanings. Frame-less meanings do not exist. Higher levels of meaning require frames of reference.

Meaning is context-sensitive both internally and externally. Ideas, thoughts, emotions, experiences, etc. can mean different things in different contexts. Internal contexts are our frames. Frames govern, modulate, drive and control our experiences. Your thoughts, feelings, language, behavior and responses are expressions of your frames.

Setting particular frames leads to certain consequences and conclusions, known as "logical fate" by Korzybski. The logical fate of your frames show up in your actions and interactions, called "Frame Games" by Hall. The "games" we play in life from our actions, relationships, talk, mental and emotional games, are functions and expressions of your frames. Like Hall says, "Where there's a frame, there's a game. Where's there's a game in play, there's a frame."

All human experiences occur within frames whether it's cultural frames-of-reference, personal frames, family frames, business and economic frames, etc. The language frames is one of the largest frames that we unconsciously live in and which governs our experiences. We have no choice about living with frames, framing, and reframing. He (or she) who sets the frame controls the interaction. Setting the frame means either setting the content or subject matter or setting the context of the subject matter.

We have the power to speak our subjective reality into being. However, we live mostly unconscious of our meanings and structures. Self-reflexive thinking is what creates the complexity and layeredness of thought-and-emotion upon thought-and-emotion and so on. We experience layers of thoughts upon thoughts and these build upon each other to create even more complex conceptual systems. Our consciousness operates simultaneously at multiple levels.

Our meanings feel real to us because they put us into state. Meanings govern the states of consciousness and even modulate both our central and autonomic nervous system. Sometimes, our meaning frames don't enhance our lives. They may be toxic and don't serve us well. It is in our best interest to run an ecology check and check our meanings to quality control them.

Here are some questions you can ask yourself:

- Does this thought, emotion, state, belief, etc. Serve me well?
- Does this enhance my life, bring out my best, and/or empower me to achieve my goals?
- Does it enable me to act in a way true to my desires?

* * *

Intention Matrix

The Meaning Matrix and the Intention Matrix share a close relationship with one another. The Intention Matrix is where you create the reasons you want something or see something a particular way. This is where we invent the meanings that make up our sense of direction and purpose. Intention refers to our higher purpose or goal. Intentionality is the ability to create a purpose and a sense of direction.

The Intention Matrix is where we map purpose, agenda, motives and all that leads to dreams, passions, and motivations. Developing intention is what allows you to do things on purpose. When we have an intention, it's like we have something in the back of our mind for why we do what we do.

We tend to map numerous and various purposes within each of the content matrices. These intentions may conflict with one another which may leave us feeling torn about what we want. All of us are full of wants, desires, and intentions. Some of these intentions come and go while others stay with us for a lifetime.

The Intention Matrix gives us a sense of meaning beyond the present moment, which lays the foundation for how we orient ourselves into the future. When we create intention, we experience the mental states of will, purpose, conation, decision, and choice. The codes and frames within our Intention Matrix shows up in our lives as motives and motivation. Every motivation has an underlying motive. Weak intentions imply weak motivation which means the underlying motive is also weak. If you try to accomplish something with a weak intention, it will be much easier for you to get thrown off track when challenges arise.

Intentionality can help us access other aspects of consciousness that often transcend everyday states. These areas include:

- Ontology: How you think about existence itself and Being-ness.
- Telology: Your awareness of life from where it came to where it's going from.
- Theology: Your thoughts about whether or not there's a higher power and about your ultimate concerns.
- Epistemology: Your thoughts about how you know what you know.

Having a weak Intention Matrix can lead to procrastination, indecision, inability to focus, among other things. In this sorry state, it will feel like your life is determined by the environment and things outside of you.

You can elicit the Intention Matrix by asking goal-oriented questions such as the following:

- What do you want?
- What are you trying to accomplish?
- What's your purpose or agenda?

Intention relates to and involves what you value, to valuing, what you consider important and meaningful as well as what you intend to do about the things you notice, feel, and experience. The Intention Matrix arises from the Meaning Matrix and is also a part of it. All of the ways you make meaning and the cognitive patterns that you use apply equally to your intentions.

Humans create and express intention in everything we do. We may want something to occur or not occur, seek to achieve or attain something, as well as develop agendas that make up our motives and motivation. This is because the Intention Matrix is a process matrix, meaning it's not about any specific type of content. It simply describes the process of wanting, intending, and valuing. From our intentionality comes all of the specific intentions we construct for each of the content matrices: self, power, time, others, and world. We have specific intentions in each matrix and sometimes they conflict with one another. Other times, they combine together to create a larger gestalt so that you feel fully aligned and congruent. As a result, your actions and sense of self is also harmonious and congruent.

The word intention comes from the latin word "intentus", which at its most basic definition means to "stretch out". Our intentions is what allows us to stretch out to what we want, what's before us, and to the direction we want to move in. Intentions organize and direct our consciousness at the primary level. The thoughts in front of our mind, or what's "on our mind", make up what we're attending to. If what we attend to and our intentions are aligned, the phenomenon of will arises. This refers to the ability to choose our responses.

Moving up the Matrix allows you to understand what you or your client truly want, what you think you are going after, and check whether or not you are actually getting your highest intentions or not. When we live intentionally, we get a sense that we are in control of, what we pay attention to, when, where, and for how long. You have a big enough "why" to govern and organize the everyday intentions and to filter out the signal from the noise.

Hall writes, "Our intention matrix not only out-frames (which is a frame above a frame) our immediate goals and objectives, but could also organize our beliefs and understandings of our ultimate purpose and perhaps even the ultimate purposes of the universe. Here you construct ideas about whether or not the universe is friendly or unfriendly, chaotic or ordered, intelligent or unintelligent, determined or open for choice, etc. In this Matrix, you create your meanings that make up concepts about all sorts of things - spirituality, philosophy, religion, ontology, etc."

We all experience multiple intentions and layers of goals. Whenever we classify something in our Meaning Matrix, we do so to "make sense" of the world. This creates our "inner logic" which is our first intention, to understand the outside world. The intention behind that is to be able to manage it, first in your mind and then to decide what to do about what's out there.

We need a well-developed Power Matrix (which we'll talk more about later) to supplement your Intention Matrix. The Power Matrix is what enables you to become intentional and take an intentional stance in life. Without sufficient resources from your Power Matrix, you won't feel like you have enough capacity or energy to translate your intentions into reality. We also have to be careful about over-emphasizing intention because this can lead to "tunnel vision" and cause us to miss what's right in front of us. We can find the right balance with intentionality by developing wisdom.

In order to detect someone's intention, ask about the why of yours or the person's intention. Ask "why is that important?" or "what are the higher values (what you think and feel as significant and important) that drive your intentions?" When you find a value, you are detecting this matrix. Values act as motives and create motivation. Your agenda is what you want. In this way, values can indicate what a person is moving toward or away from.

From a neurological perspective, intention is the part of the mind that activates your motor cortex. As a result, your intentions put you into action. If you think about anything, you will almost always feel an urge to do something. This urges comes from your intention, which in turns, stimulates an inner sense of the need to act on your thoughts. For example, if someone starts yelling at you, your intention may activate a motor program to leave and remove yourself from the situation, or it could activate a need to for you to stand your ground and start yelling back.

CHAPTER 9: THE MATRIX MODEL

Living on purpose endows your life with a sense of direction. This greatly affects your sense of Self, Power, Others, Time, and World i.e. your content matrices. Since each matrix has its own set of intentions, it would be a good idea to detect your intentions in each one. Intentions can become problematic when they're weak or ill-formed. If you don't pour enough energy into your intentions, they won't take you very far. For example, you might intend to read a few pages each day from a good book but then you keep putting it off by telling yourself that you have other things to do and as a result, you never get around to doing it.

We need to be careful of intending at the wrong level or intending impossible things. Both of these things happen frequently. This usually happens when you have an unpleasant experience and you immediately create an intention to stop having that emotion, thought, or awareness. This leads to a phenomenon known as command negation which can create seemingly paradoxical effects. There are ways to properly negate things but this is the wrong way to do it. An example of command negation would be something like "don't think of a pink elephant" or "don't get nervous". When you make statements like this towards yourself, your subconscious mind doesn't process the "don't" and instead focuses on the thing you don't want.

We can also create paradoxes by confusing logical levels. An example of this is having an emotion, and then commenting on the emotion. The comment about the emotion exists at a different logical level than the emotion itself. When we don't distinguish between the experience and the meta-comment, we create a "paradox".

* * *

Content Matrices

Self Matrix

The Self Matrix is the central conceptual matrix we all live in, operate from, and take with us everywhere we go. It's one of the first things we all construct as we grow up. It's our first classification, and by extension, the first frame we call into existence.

Your Self Matrix is called into existence as soon as your parents name you. The name is used as a summary term for you and your parents begin to relate to that. Your parents related to you as a little person with a name but you don't know this as a baby, you can only feel it. Once you become consciously aware of this, you begin to ask yourself questions like:

- Who am I? What am I?
- What is my nature, purpose, destiny, value, etc.?
- Am I loved? Am I lovable?

When creating our conceptual frame of self, we first begin by recognizing ourselves as an "I" or "me". Before we recognize ourselves as a "self", we first begin by recognizing ourselves as a living, breathing, organism. Our experience is limited to what's in our immediate environment. Naming allows us to develop thoughts and feelings about ourselves. The "Self" then becomes an object of awareness. From there, we start associating various emotional states to "self".

CHAPTER 9: THE MATRIX MODEL

As this occurs, our first meta-state, self-awareness, grows into an awareness of self with certain qualities.

We also receive various messages from parents and other adults that gives us more information about how they see us and the meanings they assign. Our sense of self in the eyes of others creates our first concept of self. As we become more self-aware and meta-state ourselves about awareness, we also receive thought-feeling states from others about ourselves. This allows us to construct our Self Matrix by layering in thoughts-and-feelings about these ideas.

From self-awareness, we get multiple other maps about ourselves. These maps include our sense of self in self-esteem, self-confidence, social self, and more. With almost any other facet of self, you create another "self". All of us have many selves. We often have many different roles we play and we can set many different emotions as meta-states about ourselves. We can identify with feelings, roles, words, concepts, etc.

How you map yourself determines everything about you. If you feel and think of yourself as someone worthwhile, you will experience a healthy Matrix. However, if you have a lot of self-hatred, then you will experience a debilitating Matrix. When a person's Self Matrix isn't well-developed, they tend to take everything personally. This is especially true when something unpleasant occurs. A weak Self Matrix can also lead to someone being primarily other-referent and will constantly seek other's validation. Your mapping or framing of your Matrix will either work for you or against you depending on whether or not it's well-formed or ill-formed. Your concepts about other people or human nature can also potentially undermine your Self Matrix if ill-formed.

The goal of working with the Self Matrix is to empower it so that it works for you instead of against you. This may include finding and updating any erroneous concepts. It also means developing a healthy relationship to the ideas of value, worth, responsibility, loveability, etc.

A healthy Self Matrix is the difference between feeling you're worthy, valuable and respectable versus seeking to experience things in the world to obtain those feelings. Achieving or not achieving a goal has no impact on your self-worth. A healthy self matrix knows how to separate person from behavior and self-esteem from self-confidence. The meaning you map about your concept of self will determine whether or not you move through the world trying to be somebody or whether you live in the world as an expression of your innate beingness.

Whenever a person is dealing with an issue, the problem is never the person but the frames they mapped for themselves. By focusing on the problem and not the person, the ego isn't on the line, therefore there's nothing to prove.

Self-confidence refers to the things that you can do such as your abilities, skills, and achievements. Unlike self-esteem, which is unconditional, self-confidence is conditional. Developing certain skills earns the right to self-confidence. Attaching the feeling of self-confidence to something you're not competent in will create problems. Your confidence is misplaced. Instead, you should focus on your strengths and find areas and tasks which you have a natural inclination so you can become highly-skilled and make the greatest contribution.

The super-ego is our sense of consciousness and is related to our sense of right and wrong as well as being and doing what's proper, ethical, honorable, and moral. It creates a consciousness in relation to others. A person with a well-developed super-ego knows how to act appropriately in a way that honors self and others.

Each of us are capable of becoming ego-involved in our beliefs, ideas, emotions, experiences, etc. This happens by over-identifying with our ego and/or by lack of healthy ego development. When we first start off in the world, our sense of self is very fragile. Over time, we learn how to develop boundaries. First, we have no ego and no boundaries. Slowly but surely, we begin to make distinctions. We use the power of "no" to establish our own space and develop our power to dis-identify with things that do not fit us and protect ourselves from them entering our world. Saying "yes" develops our power to bring ideas, experiences, people, and feelings into ourselves and welcome them as part of our world.

When you over-focus on the Self Matrix, you weaken your ability to connect with others and experience full and rich relationships. Weakness in the Self Matrix indicates a lack of sufficient and healthy independence, which is a requirement for inter-dependence with others. A weak Self Matrix can lead to co-dependency, neediness, being unable to stand up for oneself, unable to say no, etc.

You can hear the Self Matrix whenever there's a lot of talk about self and one's sense of value, confidence, identification, etc. How much of a person's talk is one's self? To activate the Self Matrix or any other Matrix, inquire about one's self:

- What do you think about yourself?

- Do you like yourself?
- Do you believe in yourself?
- Is your sense of self-esteem conditional or unconditional?

These and many other questions elicit a sense of self and activates the thoughts-and-feelings one has about those concepts. Events and experiences can do the same.

Examples

- Think about winning the lottery.
- Think about making a mistake and getting laughed at.
- Think about getting fired for an unjust reason.

Events elicit people to respond from their sense of self, this includes one's self-esteem and self-confidence. People tend not to respond effectively because they have not mapped a sufficient and adequate sense of self in these 2 dimensions.

According to Gregory Bateson, I is the biggest nominalization. This is because noun-like words point to processes, not things. Humans are living, breathing, emoting, and thinking, all at once as an ever-changing process. When a nominalization is reflexive, meaning it refers to itself, we have what Bateson calls a multi-ordinal term.

Multi-ordinal refers to the fact that it operates on multiple levels of mind. We can use the same word to think and speak at different levels and because of this, it's easy to confuse levels which leads to confusion for others and category errors. This shows up in real life when you have 2 people thinking and talking at different levels but using the same terms. The level you may be referencing involves a different concept than what the other person is thinking. Any nominalization that is reflexive can create this misunderstanding. This includes love, fear, anger, self, etc.

Since we lack the necessary terms for describing mental phenomena, we end up using the same word at different levels and mean different things. This is what we refer to as multi-ordinality. A true multi-ordinal term will mean nothing apart from its level of abstraction. To understand what it means, you have to first specify the level one is referring to. As an NLPer, you need to recognize multi-ordinal words and inquire about the level in which you or someone else is using that term.

The term self is multi-ordinal and there exists multiple layers of self. At the primary level, we speak of ourselves as a sentient being. We can refer to this self as Self1. Here, we speak of ourselves as the actor, experiencer or doer. You are grounded in your everyday state and operating in reference to the world "out there".

When we move up to the first meta-state, we speak of ourselves as the observing self, which we'll call Self2. You experience yourself as observing Self1. This self generates self-awareness, reflexive self-consciousness, and state of mind (or meta-program) of witnessing your self rather than judging or evaluating.

If you move yourself to the meta-state of taking charge of things, which is the meta-program of judger, then you can speak about yourself as the director of experience, Self3. At this level, you are operating as the director of the experiencing self (Self 1) or your observing self (Self 2). This is you running your own brain, taking charge of how you inform your goals, plans, self-definition, etc.

You can move to a meta-state above those levels and experience yourself, which we'll call Self4, where you can theorize about your previous selves. This more executive level enables you to philosophize and to think about the meaning of self and what you can become.

This process of creating higher selves can go on indefinitely. We all have the ability to create multiple higher level selves, or multiple frames of awareness of self. However, it's still the one and the same self doing. It is you thinking and feeling at various levels of mind, not different entities.

From Self3 and onwards, we have what's called infinite regress where we have thoughts and feelings about our previous thoughts and feelings. In Neuro-Semantics, it's been renamed as Infinite Progress to imply the fact that with every jump, we progress to another level of awareness, or POV, about our concept of self. Self1, Self2, Self3, etc is shorthand for saying I operate at level 1, level 2, level 3, etc. These selves explain how you experience multi-levels and dimensions of abstractions simultaneously.

* * *

Power Matrix

The feeling of power is an intimate part of your sense of self. We experience our sense of power in states of self-confidence and self-efficacy. First, we develop a sense of power, then we develop a sense of what we can do. The Power Matrix is arguably one of the most important content matrices. According to developmental psychology, a baby's first mapping is about his or herself. Immediately afterwards, the baby begins to map what it can do. We create maps about whether or not we have the resources, capability, or power, to deal with the world as it is.

Some of our first felt questions are questions about power:

- Can I handle myself in this situation?
- Can I manage my mind and emotions?
- Can I take effective action?

As we create frames about power and capabilities, these frames involve aspects of our sense of self called self-efficacy and self-confidence. These frames refer to our ability to trust our mind-emotion system in being able to effectively handle the challenges of life, and the confidence that you place in yourself regarding your abilities and aptitudes.

Take a moment to consider the meanings you've formulated about power and the concept of power:

- Can I handle myself in this situation?
- Can I manage my own mind and emotions?
- Can I take effective action?

How you conceptualize these questions play a part in your overall self-definitions regarding your abilities, capabilities, and potential. They make up the key frames of your Power Matrix.

The Power Matrix also answers fundamental questions about you and your life:

- What can I do?
- What skills and resources can I develop?
- Can I cope with things?

Your sense of power correlates with your sense of being resourceful which can make all the difference in dealing with the world. A well-developed Power Matrix allows you to take ownership of your thoughts, feelings, and emotions. It also allows you to be "response-able" as a proactive person who takes initiative. It's also the foundation for many desirable states including resiliency, strength, courage, etc.

If you grew up in a nurturing environment, then you probably have a good relationship with power. Ideally, you would have parents who supported you and nurtured your powers. They would've also encouraged you to experiment and made it safe to explore using your new powers as they emerged. The world would seem safe to you as you developed your emotional, verbal and behavioral powers.

On the other hand, if you grew up in a dysfunctional family and culture, then you likely have a bad relationship to power. You probably see the world as dangerous and would've concluded that the world isn't a safe place. You would've undermined your sense of power by setting frames about response powers as "weak, fragile, impossible, etc."

Whatever frames you construct from your experiences will be the governing frames today of your Power Matrix. Your frames create self-fulfilling prophecies. Not only will you be conditioned to think a certain way, but you'll feel that "this is the way it is" whether that's feeling powerful or powerless. No matter how painful or unpleasant an event might be, it's still just an event. What matters is the frame the person builds from those events. The frames are always the problem, never the person or event.

Our human powers arise from and are expressed in the 4 basic powers which you can use to make things happen in your world. 2 of them are private and 2 are public responses. Our thinking and feeling responses make up our 2 private and internal powers. We have mental (think, imagine, remember, etc.) and emotional (feel, and to register values and meanings in your body) powers. Our speaking and acting responses make up our 2 public powers. We have verbal powers (speech and language) and behavioral powers (action, gesture, and movement).

These 4 powers give us a wide range of things we can do in response to people, events, and situations. You can always think and feel, and you can usually speak and act. By recognizing these powers as skills, we can develop our mental, emotional, verbal, and behavioral competencies in responding. You can become more skillful, resourceful, and effective in the ways which you can influence. Discovering these powers will help you develop greater self-confidence.

By recognizing the 4 powers as skills, we can develop our mental, emotional, verbal, and behavioral competencies in responding. You can become more skillful, useful, resourceful, and effective in the ways in which you can influence. Discovering these powers will help you develop greater self-confidence.

Your IQ is developed by using your thinking-feeling powers. Your thinking-feeling helps you develop the basic skills of understanding and then finding, developing, and using effective strategies as you live your day to day life. Your EQ also plays a role because you have to deal with your emotions as you learn. You have to develop awareness of what you feel, accepting those feelings, and managing them well.

Your Power Matrix can be activated by anything that challenges you or provokes a response out of you. Sometimes, any and all stimuli in life can elicit this Matrix and invite you to do something in response to the trigger. Most people tend to be reactive than proactive. In other words, most people react instead of mindfully responding. It is the mindfulness of "running your own brain" that allows you to take charge of these powers.

To become proactive, first begin by creating meaning frames to validate the idea of accessing your personal powers, taking effective action, investing your time and effort into something you care about, and the like. These meaning frames will allow you to operate with a healthy respect to power. Start by accepting your fallibility. Realize that you cannot, and will not, become all-powerful or skilled in everything nor do you need to. Most of us are incompetent at a great many things. Focusing on what you can't do will only make yourself miserable and creates an impoverished mental map.

CHAPTER 9: THE MATRIX MODEL

To create an enhancing map, focus on what you care about and your strengths. At the same time, find and cultivate your aptitudes and talents. By focusing on what you can do and what you can develop even more skill in, you develop confidence in yourself around an area of competency. This gives us the basis of feeling good and enjoying something. It also provides the basis of being passionate about something that you can then use to make a living and even become financially independent.

Beware of over-relying on your strengths. They may leak into other domains of life where they prove less than effective. Your strengths and aptitudes don't make you a worthwhile person. You're a worthwhile person just because. What you do in terms of skills, gifts, contributions, etc. is a different facet of life.

When you talk about what to do, how to do, and when to do something, you're speaking from the Power Matrix. You can detect someone's Power Matrix by calibrating to their state. Watch for when a person seems out of it, or unresourceful as well as when a person is resourceful, in the zone, and able to respond effectively.

* * *

Others Matrix

The Others Matrix includes all of the specific content you have about others, human nature as a whole, sociology, politics, and anthropology. This matrix deals with your social self and how you relate to others. Humans are social creatures and part of our identity is formed by how we relate to other people. We can construct maps in this matrix that either enable us or disable us in regards to how we get along and we relate to others. It reflects and influence how you feel loved or not, creating alliances/partnerships, falling in love, supporting others, and more.

This Matrix answers numerous questions of how you think about others in your world like:

- Who are other people?
- What kind of map do you have about mankind or people in general and specifically?
- What do you think and feel about certain groups of people e.g. religion, politics, socioeconomic, etc.

Your Others Matrix is a reflection of how you mapped and developed meanings about what you understand, believe, and expect of people. It refers to what you think and feel about others. The Others Matrix also includes fictitious people such as from TV shows and movies. It even includes people who are already dead. Within this matrix, you experience the results of your beliefs and attitudes regarding your philosophies about human nature.

CHAPTER 9: THE MATRIX MODEL

When we first arrive on this planet, our survival depends entirely on other people. We're also born without an individuated sense of self. Our psychological development takes several years and this allows us to separate from others and become independent and autonomous.

You can detect the Others Matrix by noticing how someone gets along with other people. Ask questions about how a person deals with interpersonal behaviors and emotions like love, support, affection, friendship, betrayal, etc. You can also look to social meta-programs and patterns for rapport, persuasion, leadership, and so on. Our Others Matrix makes up a large part of our Emotional Intelligence. Any cues or signals of EQ or lack thereof are signs of this Matrix.

The meanings you give to people will determine whether or not you turn to others when your energy levels are low and you need to recharge your batteries. This is known in NLP as the Extraversion Meta-Program. If, however, you turn inward to recharge, then you have the Introversion Meta-Program. If you mapped both as valuable and significant, then you have the Ambivert Meta-Program.

How your Others Matrix is initially formed has a profound effect on all of your social skills and experiences. This Matrix arises from how you understood the first people you interacted with and how they treated you. They tend to function as prototypes for numerous conceptual categories for you.

Your parents or guardians often act as your most fundamental prototypes for masculine-feminine relationships. They were also the first people you dealt with as authority figures. In addition, they offered you a prototype for how humans handle emotions, relationships, conflicts, love, trust, etc.

We can't help but define ourselves by the reflection we see of ourselves in the eyes of those around us. In other words, we see ourselves in terms of how we think other people see us. From our experiences with others, we create a social panorama in our mind consisting of various representations of good and bad people, close ones and strangers, friendly and unfriendly people, and so on. We internalize others and carry those representations around inside of us which we embed in multiple layered frames.

Your Others Matrix is directly related to and influenced by your Self Matrix. At one point, your Self Matrix and Others Matrix were one and the same. It was through growth and development that you became independent. Independence allows you to stand on your own 2 feet and engage in healthy interdependent relationships.

*　*　*

Time Matrix

Time is just a mental construct. It doesn't exist at the level of experience. We construct our understanding of time from the events that we experience in our lives. Events exist in the outside world and from those events we create "time". We create time by comparing one event to another event. We compare events that have happened, to events that are happening, to those that will happen in the future. We're able to compare events using constancy of representation. We can hold multiple mental images in our head at once. Events occur at the primary level and when we step up to compare and contrast them, we create time at a meta-level. All conceptual time is "meta-time".

Our ability to construct time allows us to live in different time zones (past, present and future) and to direct your attention to those different directions. Time zones also relate to what level of mind you experience events. If we're at the primary level and we tend to get lost in the moment, we're "in time" so to speak. This is also known as the flow state. We can also experience events from a meta-level and have awareness of an event in relation to other events. Those who live on a meta-level to time are out of time or through-time.

The person who's primarily "in time" tends not to regard time as important. Their main priority is moving from one event to another and being present to each person or experience. In-time has the potential to conflict with meta-time. This can happen when someone is primarily in-time yet they still have to manage deadlines, schedule events, and ensure things get done when they should. This conflict involves the feeling of knowing you should arrive on time and and get things done in a timely manner, in other words, "paying more attention to time", when you just want to be lost in time.

We can map the meta-programs distinctions in-time and through-time. These 2 generate different experiences of time: sequential time and random time. Sequential time allows you to filter temporal information so that you know when to do something and for how long. This is especially useful for being punctual, meeting deadlines, working from a time schedule, etc. In random time, you let go of your awareness of time. You completely lose track of it and in that instant, you don't care.

In-time and through-time are both valuable in certain areas and problematic in others. If you can use through-time and in-time effectively, then you have a healthy relationship to time. If you can live in the present, keep your eye on the future, and use the past for learning, then you have a great time management strategy for all the events in your life.

A well-formed time-line allows you to experience an overall sense of perspective about your entire life which can help support you in maintaining emotional well-being and balance. The meanings you give to time will greatly influence many of your emotions and influences your skills and performance. If you see time as a friend, then you will see it as something to recognize and embrace. However, if you see time as an enemy, then you will see it as something to fend off. What you believe about time also affects how you map the other matrices of self, power, others, and world.

Unless you work in a profession with a strong orientation to the past, it is generally ideal to have a present-day focus with an eye towards the future. The past is useful for learning and for grounding resources. Apart from that, it serves no purpose. And it doesn't even exist. This means that there's no such thing as "unfinished business". If it's in the past, then it's done. If it's not finished in your mind, then it is going on right now in your mind which means it's something you can finish today.

Overemphasizing the past as determining factors over your mind and body emotional states creates dis-empowerment. Over-valuing your future causes you to focus on what doesn't exist. If the past doesn't exist, that means we can change the past to our liking. Technically speaking, we can have a happy childhood anytime we want. We don't even remember the past accurately to begin with. There are many NLP patterns to help you with changing the past such as the Phobia Cure, Decision Destroyer, and various Time-lining processes.

According to Steve Andreas, a prominent NLPer, the way you use examples in the different time frames of past, present, and future has a profound impact on the degree to which your sense of self will continue over time. You can discover this for yourself by asking yourself "How big is my present?" If it's a tiny point where the past and future meet, then you're going to have a hard time experiencing yourself in the now.

One of the best ways to control or predict the future is to create the person you're becoming, and the experiences you're having. This swishes your brain in that direction and sets in motion a self-fulfilling prophecy that will self-organize the rest of your mind-body-emotion system. As a result, it integrates your Intentional Matrix with your Time Matrix. You can enrich your past, present, and future with more resources by future-pacing yourself with the quality and skills you want and putting them into your future time-line. From there, you can increase them until they pull you into that bright future.

When you're caught up in a state due to its intensity, repetitiveness, or persistence, (state-dependence) your mind may unconsciously activate a memory based on a similar experience. Your state can help you pull evidence and proof from previous experiences that support your current state. When state-dependency activates a past search for reinforcement in that matter, it creates a self-fulfilling prophecy.

* * *

World Matrix

The world matrix contains the content of all the different worlds you know about, navigate through, and care about. Your mind has separate understandings for the world in general and the many worlds within worlds. This matrix makes up what you know about the external environment and what you mapped so far. It represents everything outside of yourself in all of the contexts or worlds which you act and relate.

The world matrix creates the logical level of the background knowledge in your mind. It makes up your worldview and your general philosophy about politics, economics, and the like, and your general theological views about God, the universe, what life is, where it came from and what's it all about. The world matrix answers questions like whether or not we think the world is friendly or unfriendly, abundant or scarce, dangerous or exciting, and how X (where X means a specific world) works. Common worlds include business, work, politics, culture, law, etc.

When you develop a self, you have a self in a particular context or world, which goes to show how influential the World Matrix is on the Self Matrix. Ego-strength is a term coined by L. Michael Hall which refers to your ability to adjust effectively to life's challenges. Having a high ego-strength allows you to deal with the unpleasant aspects of the world around you, or in life in general, using your internal and external resources.

We have various types of intelligences that allows us to deal effectively with different worlds. For example, IQ (Intelligence Quotient) enables you to adjust well to the changing times culturally and economically. EQ (Emotional Quotient) intelligences allows you to make the appropriate adjustments in the world of relationships. SQ (Spiritual Quotient) intelligence facilitates your adjustment to the world of meaning such as inspiration and spirituality.

The World Matrix governs all of your social, political, economic, business, career, and racial worlds. A well-developed world matrix will lead you to care about and want to express competence in the domains that make up your life-world. You may want to express your competence in business and career, groups, sports, etc. All sorts of opportunities become available when you have well-developed meanings in your World Matrix. On the other hand, if you map fearful, impoverished, limiting meanings in your World Matrix, then any given world can become a frightful and intimidating place.

As we live our lives, there will be many opportunities for us to engage and experience new facets of reality. This expands your World Matrix and by extension your worldview to keep growing and expanding, which is a good thing. All worlds are fluid and dynamic. In order to deal with fluidity around us, our maps must also continue to change. You must also be careful of overindentifying with one particular world, which will cause your life to get out of balance.

Some of the first questions we ask as we're growing up are "what's the world like?" or "what's out there?" As we answer those questions, we create models of the world to figure the world out. Usually, our models of the world are erroneous and are created with a child's mind and with first impressions that can have a lasting impact on our thinking. We never deal with the outside world, only our model of the world. We can only experience the world through our senses and maps. If you find the world is negative, the problem isn't the world, but your map of the world.

Your world matrix becomes active once you engage in one of the many worlds. To detect any particular World Matrix, ask questions about a person's world or worlds:

- What worlds do you live in?
- What worlds would you like to deal with?
- Do you seek to mostly to adapt the world to you (Judger) or do you seek mostly to adapt to the world (Perceiver)?
- Do you seek first the sensory-based facts of the world or do you seek to intuit patterns and meanings in the world?

Finding the right balance in engaging with the outside world is key. If you can effectively cope with the world and even master it, then you will feel successful and self-confident. However, if you overemphasize the outside, then you may become oriented to success, competition, winning, and external status symbols of success. You may become more shallow as a person as the external world becomes more important.

Chapter 10: NLP Certifications

SNLP

The first certification board to exist is The Society of NLP or SNLP for short. They were founded by Richard Bandler and John Grinder, the co-founders of NLP, and they're still active to this day.

Here are their requirements for the Practitioner Level:

- Behavioral integration of the basic presuppositions of NLP:
- The ability to change the process by which we experience reality is more often valuable than changing the content of our experience of reality.
- The meaning of your communication is the response you get.
- All distinctions human beings are able to make concerning our environment and our behavior can be usefully represented through the visual, auditory, kinesthetic, olfactory, and gustatory senses.
- The resources an individual needs to effect a change are already within them. The map is not the territory.

- The positive worth of the individual is held constant, while the value and appropriateness of the internal and/or external behavior is questioned.
- There is a positive intention motivating every behavior; and a context in which every behavior has value.
- Feedback vs. Failure - All results and behaviors are achievements, whether they are desired results for a given task/context or not.
- Rapport Establishment & Maintenance
- Verbal & Nonverbal Pacing & Leading
- Verbal and Nonverbal Elicitation of Responses
- Calibrating through Sensory Experience
- Representational Systems (Sensory Predicates and Accessing Cues)
- Milton Model, Meta Model
- Elicitation of Well-Formed Goals, Direction, and Present State
- Overlapping and Translating Representational Systems
- Eliciting, Installing & Utilizing Anchors in all sensory systems
- Ability To Shift Consciousness
- Sub-modalities (utilizing including Timelines, Belief Change, Swish Patterns, etc.)
- Omni Directional Chunking
- Accessing and Building Resources
- Content & Context Reframing
- Creating & Utilizing Metaphors
- Strategy Detection, Elicitation, Utilization, And Installation
- Demonstration of Flexibility of Behavior and Attitude

Here are their requirements for the Master Practitioner Level:

- Behavioral competency in all Practitioner level skills and the demonstration to do several of these simultaneously.
- The ability to design behavioral flexibility and attitudes that produce specific results with self and others.
- Minimum ability to identify and utilize the Master Practitioner skills, techniques, and patterns linguistically:
- Changing Beliefs
- Eliciting & Utilizing Meta-Programs
- Criteria:
- Identification of and Utilization of Criteria
- Adjusting Criteria
- Sleight of Mouth Patterns
- Deliberate multilevel communication
- Stacking Realities
- Timeline Patterns
- Stacking Presuppositions
- Temporal/Spatial Predicates
- Negotiating
- Propulsion Systems
- Installing Strategies
- Threshold Pattern
- Breaking Generalizations & Building New Ones
- Rapid Inductions, Deep Trance Phenomena
- Deep Trance Identification
- Demonstrated ability to do change work with self and other

Their requirements for the Trainer and Master Trainer level is not publicly available at the time of writing this book.

IBCP

The International Board of Coaches and Practitioners, or, IBCP was founded by NLP Master Trainer Michael Stevenson, who is also the founder of Transform Destiny, a prominent NLP training school.

His certification board is reasonably priced and comes with a host of benefits such as a digital certificate with click-able verification of your credentials, listing on the NLP, Hypnosis, and Coaching referral directory, one ticket to the annual IBCP convention, and much more.

Here are IBCP's standards for each certification taken from their website:

Practitioner of NLP, Hypnotherapy, TIME Techniques, Success and Life Coaching, EFT

Duration of training: Minimum of 120 hours of training in the basics of NLP, hypnosis and/or TIME Techniques patterns taught by a Certified Master Trainer or a Certified Trainer, with exercises under the direct supervision of a duly certified Master Trainer, a Trainer, or a Master Practitioner under the Master Trainer's or Trainer's guidance required. The three trainings and hours can run concurrently.

Method of Training: Training is either to be held live, in-person with direct supervision and evaluation of students in exercises, or through online, recorded video training with verification of hours and direct supervision of the student doing exercises, either through recorded exercises with a volunteer, or live evaluation by the trainer over video chat.

Demonstration of ability to identify the following basic skills, techniques, patterns, and concepts of NLP and to utilize them competently with self and with others.

Behavioral integration of the basic presuppositions of NLP, including:

- Outcome orientation with respect for others' models of the world and the ecology of the system
- Distinction between map and territory
- There is only feedback (cybernetic)-no failure
- Meaning of your communication is the response you get
- Adaptive intent of all behavior
- Everyone has the necessary resources to succeed
- Resistance is a signal of insufficient pacing
- Law of requisite variety
- Rapport, establishment and maintenance of
- Pacing and Leading (verbal and non-verbal)
- Calibration (sensory-based experience)
- Representational systems (predicates, and accessing cues)
- Meta-Model
- Milton-Model
- Elicitation of well-formed, ecological outcomes and structures of present state.
- Overlap and Translation
- Metaphor creation and delivery

- Frames; contrast, relevancy, As If, Backtrack
- Anchoring (VAK)
- Collapse Anchors
- Chain Anchors
- Ability to shift consciousness to external or internal, as required by the moment's task
- Dissociation and Association
- Chunking
- Sub-modalities
- Verbal and non-verbal elicitation of responses
- Accessing and building of resources
- Reframing
- Parts Integration
- Strategies; detection, elicitation, utilization, & installation
- Demonstration of behavioral flexibility
- Hypnosis induction (Hypnosis)
- Deepening techniques (Hypnosis)
- Direct suggestion (Hypnosis)
- Timeline elicitation (TIME Techniques)
- Discovery of root cause (TIME Techniques)
- Eliminating negative emotions (TIME Techniques)
- Eliminating limiting decisions (TIME Techniques)
- Changing direction of the timeline (TIME Techniques)
- Putting a single SMART goal into the future (TIME Techniques)

Master Practitioner of NLP, Master Hypnotherapist, Master of TIME Techniques, and Master of Success and Life Coaching

Prerequisite: Successfully passed NLP Practitioner in accordance with the above standards.

Duration of Training: Minimum of 120 hours of advanced training taught by a Certified Master Trainer or a Certified Trainer with exercises under the direct supervision of a duly certified Master Trainer, a Trainer, or a Master Practitioner under the Master Trainer's or Trainer's guidance required. The four trainings and hours can run concurrently.

Method of Training: Trainings are only to be held live, in-person with direct supervision and evaluation of students in exercises. Virtual, distance-learning, or home-study courses are not approved under any circumstances.

Demonstration of the ability to identify the following basic skills, techniques patterns and concepts of NLP and to utilize these competently with self and with others.

- All practitioner-level skills, singly and in combination
- Design individualized interventions (generative and remedial)
- Ecological change work
- Shifting easily back and forth between content and form, and experience and label.
- Specific Master Practitioner Skills/Techniques:
- Quantum Linguistics or equivalent
- Meta Programs, elicitation, and utilization
- Basic
- Complex
- Criteria (Values):
- Identification and utilization
- Criteria ladder
- Elicitation of complex equivalence and adjustment of criteria

- Values adjustment and installation
- Spiral Dynamics values
- Installation and utilization of strategies
- Advanced use of sub-modalities
- Advanced use of Anchors (Sliding Anchors)
- Advanced Parts Integration
- Deliberate multi-level communication
- Negotiation
- Advanced communication skills
- Modeling with output
- Utilization and transformation of beliefs and advanced use of presuppositions
- Logical Levels of Therapy
- Sleight of Mouth patterns
- Compulsion Blowout
- Allergy Model
- Godiva Chocolate Pattern
- Designer Swish Patterns
- Family Therapy model
- Advanced Strategies
- TOTE Model
- Design
- Installation
- Utilization and transformation of beliefs and presuppositions
- Advanced ideomotor response, such as pendulum (Hypnosis)
- Modeling
- Detailed Personal History (TIME Techniques)
- Personal Breakthrough Session format (TIME Techniques)
- Emotional chains (TIME Techniques)
- Time-line regression (TIME Techniques)

Trainer of NLP, Trainer of Hypnotherapy, Trainer of TIME Techniques, Trainer of Life/Success Coaching, Trainer of EFT

Prerequisites: Successfully passed NLP Practitioner and NLP Master Practitioner in accordance with the above standards

Duration of Training: Minimum of 120 hours of advanced training taught by a certified Master Trainer.

Method of Training: Trainings are only to be held live, in-person with direct supervision and evaluation of students in exercises. Virtual, distance-learning or home-study courses are not approved under any circumstances.

Satisfactory demonstration of the following behavioral competencies:

- Complete behavioral competence in all Practitioner and Master Practitioner level skills, ability to do any and all practitioner and master practitioner techniques simultaneously both overtly and covertly
- Demonstrate facility to shift between content and form (IE: between experience and labeling)
- Ability to demonstrate the behavior of what one is teaching and to teach what one is doing — and to label it linguistically (IE: Model Self)
- Demonstration of Presentation and Teaching skills:
- Pacing and leading
- Respect for audience (i.e. at least keeping separate your and others model of the world, and responding to these congruently; considering and responding ecologically to others; conscious and

unconscious processes.
- Ability to answer questions, (including discerning the level and intent of questions and generating level-appropriate responses)
- Design of presentation: At the least, setting opening and closing frames, setting outcomes, chunking and sequencing of information and experience, balancing information–giving and occasions for discovery, facilitating generalization of in formation and skills across context and time
- Design of exercises: At the least, providing for both overt and covert learning in each exercise, including previously learned material for cumulative learning, specifying outcomes of exercises, providing a task for all involved persons insuring behavioral learning, including a future pace
- Explanation of exercises including the ability to explain an exercise behaviorally without the use of notes or printed aids
- Use of deep and shallow metaphor
- Utilization of multi-level feedback: ongoing re-evaluation and incorporation of overt and covert information from individuals and group
- Graceful intervention in groups: at the least maintaining rapport and giving specific sensory grounded feedback, via questions that directionalize appropriate search to facilitate people's discovery for themselves, demonstration, or if necessary, overtly telling them what to do
- "Tasking": creating a task that presupposes that a person behaves in a different way that expands his/her model of the world
- Ability to do demonstrations
- Demonstration of a personal style, and artistry (indicating that the new trainer is integrating skills into his/her own behavior)
- Demonstration of an understanding of the process of NLP Practitioner and Master Practitioner training

- Ability to demonstrate and teach all certification requirements for Hypnotherapist, Practitioner of Hypnotherapy and Master Practitioner of Hypnotherapy levels (Hypnosis)
- Demonstration of an understanding of the process of Hypnotherapy, Practitioner of Hypnotherapy and Master Hypnotherapy training. (Hypnosis)
- Ability to demonstrate and teach all certification requirements for Practitioner TIME Techniques and Master Practitioner TIME Techniques training. (TIME Techniques)
- Ability to lead groups through all TIME Techniques processes, with the exception of Emotional Chains (TIME Techniques)
- Demonstration of an understanding of the process of Practitioner TIME Techniques and Master Practitioner TIME Techniques training (TIME Techniques)

Master Trainer of NLP, Master Trainer of Hypnotherapy, Master Trainer of TIME Techniques, Master Trainer of Life/Success Coaching, Master Trainer of EFT

Prerequisites: Successfully passed NLP Practitioner, NLP Master Practitioner, and NLP Trainer in accordance with the above standards.

Duration of Training: Variable, depending on the development and progress of the subject

Satisfactory achieve the following, as mentored and evaluated by a duly certified Master Trainer of NLP:

Complete behavioral competence in all Practitioner, Master Practitioner, and Trainer level skills, ability to do any and all practitioner and master practitioner techniques without scripts simultaneously both overtly and covertly.

Adequately, competently, and clearly be able to teach NLP Practitioner, NLP Master Practitioner, and NLP Trainer Training content.

Embody all of the NLP Principles both consciously and unconsciously and use NLP in your own life (walk the talk).

Read and demonstrate competency in the 12 foundational books of NLP:

- The Structure of Magic Vol 1
- The Structure of Magic Vol 2
- Patterns of the Hypnotic Techniques of Milton H. Erickson MD Vol 1
- Patterns of the Hypnotic Techniques of Milton H. Erickson MD Vol 2
- Frogs into Princes
- NLP Vol 1
- Reframing
- Using Your Brain... For a Change
- Tranceformations
- Magic In Action
- Change Your Mind and Keep the Change
- Heart of the Mind

Assist and receive hands-on training in the following trainings (post-Trainers Training)

- Minimum one NLP Practitioner Training
- Minimum one NLP Master Practitioner Training
- Minimum three NLP Trainers Trainings

Successfully train at minimum 100 students in NLP Practitioner (over at minimum three separate trainings) and 50 students (over at minimum two separate trainings) NLP Master Practitioner following all the standards set forth by the IBCP

Create and demonstrate on original NLP technique created by the subject, either by:

- Modeling and creating a new pattern from the model
- Synthesizing NLP principles into a novel technique.

* * *

ABH-NLP

ABH-NLP was founded in 1982 by Dr. A. M. Krasner as the California Board of Hypnotherapy. Due to its rapid growth, it went on to become the American Board of Hypnotherapy with members all across the globe.

They later expanded to include NLP and their members are globally recognized for maintaining a high standard of excellence in their NLP training.

Here are their standards for each of the main certifications:

NLP Practitioner

Duration of Training: Minimum of 120 hours of training in the basics of NLP patterns taught by a Certified Trainer, or a certified Master Practitioner under the supervision of a trainer.

Demonstration of ability to identify the following basic skills, techniques, patterns and concepts of NLP and to utilize them competently with self and with others.

1. Behavioral integration of the basic presuppositions of NLP, including:
2. Outcome orientation with respect for others' models of the world and the ecology of the system.
3. Distinction between map and territory.
4. There is only feedback (cybernetic)-no failure.
5. Meaning of your communication is the response you get.
6. Adaptive intent of all behavior.
7. Everyone has the necessary resources to succeed.
8. Resistance is a signal of insufficient pacing.
9. Law of requisite variety.
10. Rapport, establishment and maintenance of.
11. Pacing and Leading (verbal and non-verbal).
12. Calibration (sensory-based experience).
13. Representational systems (predicates, and accessing cues).

14. Meta-Model.
15. Milton-Model.
16. Elicitation of well-formed, ecological outcome and structures of present state.
17. Overlap and Translation.
18. Metaphor creation.
19. Frames; contrast, relevancy, As If, Backtrack.
20. Anchoring (VAK).
21. Anchoring Techniques (contextualized to the field of application).
22. Ability to shift consciousness to external or internal, as required by the moment's task.
23. Dissociation and Association.
24. Chunking.
25. Sub-modalities.
26. Verbal and non-verbal elicitation of responses.
27. Accessing and building of resources.
28. Reframing.
29. Strategies; detection, elicitation, utilization, & installation.
30. Demonstration of behavioral flexibility.

NLP Master Practitioner

Duration of Training: Minimum of 120 hours of advanced training taught by a certified trainer. A minimum of 15 hours of direct trainer supervision.

Demonstration of the ability to identify the following basic skills, techniques patterns and concepts of NLP and to utilize these competently with self and with others:

- All practitioner-level skills, singly and in combination.
- Design individualized interventions (generative and remedial).
- Ecological change work.
- Shifting easily back and forth between content and form, and experience and label.
- Specific Master Practitioner Skills:
- Meta Programs.
- Criteria (Values).
- identification and utilization.
- criteria ladder.
- elicitation of complex equivalence and adjustment of criteria.
- sleight of mouth.
- Installation and utilization of strategies.
- Refined use of submodalities.
- Deliberate multi-level communication.
- Negotiations.
- Presentation skills.
- Modeling.
- Utilization and transformation of beliefs and presuppositions.

NLP Trainer

Duration of Training: Minimum of 120 hours of advanced training taught by a certified Master Trainer. A minimum of 15 hours of direct trainer supervision.

Satisfactory demonstration of the following behavioral competencies:

- Complete behavioral competence in all Practitioner and Master

Practitioner level skills, ability to do any and all practitioner and master practitioner techniques simultaneously both overtly and covertly.
- Demonstrate facility to shift between content and form (IE: between experience and labeling).
- Ability to do (demonstrate the behavior of) what one is teaching and to teach what one is doing — and to label it linguistically (IE: Model Self).
- Demonstration of Presentation and Teaching skills:
- Pacing and leading.
- Respect for audience (i.e. at least keeping separate your and others model of the world, and responding to these congruently; considering and responding ecologically to others; conscious and unconscious processes.
- Ability to answer questions, (including discerning the level and intent of questions and generating level-appropriate responses).
- Design of presentation: At the least, setting opening and closing frames, setting outcomes, chunking and sequencing of information and experience, balancing information–giving and occasions for discovery, facilitating generalization of information and skills across context and time.
- Design of exercises: At the least, providing for both overt and covert learning in each exercise, including previously learned material for cumulative learning, specifying outcomes of exercises, providing a task for all involved persons insuring behavioral learning, including a future pace.
- Explanation of exercises including the ability to explain an exercise behaviorally without the use of notes or printed aids.
- Use of deep and shallow metaphor.
- Utilization of multi-level feedback: ongoing re-evaluation and incorporation of overt and covert information from individuals

and group.
- Graceful intervention in groups: at the least maintaining rapport and giving specific sensory grounded feedback, via questions that directionalize appropriate search to facilitate peoples discovery for themselves, demonstration, or if necessary, overtly telling them what to do.
- "Tasking": creating of a task that presupposes that a person behave in a different way that expands his/her model of the world.
- Ability to do demonstrations.
- Demonstration of a personal style, and artistry (indicating that the new trainer is integrating skills into his/her own behavior).
- Demonstration of an understanding of the process of NLP Practitioner and Master Practitioner NLP training.

NLP Master Trainer

Duration of Trainings: A minimum of 5 years as lead trainer in Practitioner and Master Practitioner Trainings taught as a Certified Trainer. A minimum of 5 consecutive years, member of ABNLP at the NLP trainer level. A minimum of 5 (five) Trainers Training coaching and assisting under direct trainer supervision by a Master Trainer approved by ABNLP. An evaluation of the candidate's student is also necessary. A copy of your course curriculum and course manual at Practitioner, Master Practitioner, and NLP Trainer level. A copy of Master Trainer program from your school and/or Master Trainer.

Satisfactory demonstration of the following behavioral competencies:

- A video of you teaching an NLP Practitioner and Master Practi-

tioner course, along with exercises
- Teaching at least 10 Practitioner and 10 Master Practitioner trainings
- Immediate and flawless recall and teaching of any NLP subject from memory without notes
- Being able to conduct on request and without notice a Demo Day during the NLP Trainers Training and Evaluation under direct Master Trainer supervision.
- There are additional requirements that are more subjective, and which can be discussed with your Master Trainer.

To be certified as a Master Trainer, the Trainer must be approved by 2 Master Trainers from different organizations who are current and approved members of ABNLP to provide NLP Training.

* * *

INLPTA

The INLPTA was formed in 1993 by 3 NLP Master Trainers: Wyatt Woodsmall, Marvin Oka, and Bert Feustel. It is an international cooperative association of NLP Trainers and Master Trainers who have agreed to abide by and uphold INLPTA's standards of quality, professionalism and ethics in their NLP accreditation trainings and in the conduct of their NLP business.

They have trainers in over 50 countries and on all 5 continents.

Here are their standards for each of the main certifications:

NLP Practitioner

Duration of training: Minimum of 130 hours (excluding breaks longer than 30 minutes) and a minimum of 15 days of formal course training. 18 days is recommended.

The most critical factor in evaluating practitioners is their ability to:

- Work within an outcome frame
- Establish and maintain states of resourcefulness
- Sort by others
- Establish and maintain rapport
- Respect and pace other people's models of the world
- Do effective and ecological change work

Certification requirements are the successful completion of the following:

- Written examination for intellectual competence
- Behavioral examination for behavioral competence
- Case study documentation or personal/professional application project report

CHAPTER 10: NLP CERTIFICATIONS

The assessment criteria of an INLPTA NLP Practitioner is based on Attitude (embodiment of the presuppositions of NLP), Content Knowledge (frames, principles, techniques, and distinctions) and behavioral skills (demonstrated integration of learnings)

NLP Master Practitioner

Training Structure

- Trained by an INLPTA registered NLP Trainer
- The certification training meets INLPTA training structure requirements
- Minimum of 130 hours of formal course room training. (excluding breaks longer than 30 minutes)
- Minimum of 15 days of formal course room training
- The attended training meets the INLPTA accreditation competency standards and guidelines
- The candidate has successfully met the competency standards of INLPTA of NLP Master-Practitioner, as assessed by the registered INLPTA Trainer
- The certificate needs to be signed by at least one INLPTA NLP Trainer. 2 is ideal.
- The certificates need to have the starting and ending dates, as well as the numbers of hours and dates written on them. All certificates need to ordered by the international or national INLPTA coordinator and be numbered and sealed with the official INLPTA seal.

Certification Requirements

- Behavioral competency in all Practitioner level skills and the demonstrated ability to do several patterns simultaneously
- The ability to identify, utilize and demonstrate one's integration of the Master Practitioner content, skills, frames, concepts, principles, processes, techniques and distinctions. (see INLPTA Master Practitioner Assessment Criteria list)
- The ability to do individualized interventions
- Demonstrated ability to operate from an ecological framework and philosophy, and to do ecological change work with self and others
- Advanced development of flexibility with ones' own representational systems and perceptual filters
- Demonstrated capacity to shift back and forth between content and form as appropriate to context
- Ability to track shifts in different logical levels of internal processing and logical types of descriptions
- Ability to facilitate one's own learning processes at the appropriate logical levels
- Embodiment of the Presuppositions of NLP
- Multi- tracking abilities
- Ability to maintain resourceful states for intellectual, emotional, and physical choice
- Ability to process one's own modeling of the world and to re-organize one's processing as appropriate to the context and outcome

Assessment Criteria for NLP Master Practitioner

- Degree of integration, mastery, and elegance with all NLP Practitioner Skills

- Degree of integration of NLP Master Practitioner Process Skills
- Conscious/Unconscious Embodiment of the Legs of NLP
- Conscious/Unconscious Embodiment of the Presuppositions of NLP
- Conscious/Unconscious Multi-tracking:
- Multi Layered Outcomes
- Multi-Level Calibration Skills
- Multi-Level Conscious/Unconscious Processing
- Ability to Be At Choice With the Process of Identification and Self Evaluation
- Precision Resourcefulness Through All Representational Systems
- Scope of Sensory Flexibility
- Perceptual Sorting Flexibility (Metaprograms and Perceptual Positions)
- Ability to Track One's Own Epistemological Processing
- Ability to Track the Epistemology of Others
- Epistemological Flexibility
- Ability to Track Logical Levels and Logical Typings
- Ability to Process Learning from Achievement
- Ability to Establish and Maintain Multiple levels of Rapport
- Ability to Separate Process from Content About Process
- Ability to Deliver Deliberate Multi-Level Communications
- Ability to Deliver Deliberate Multi-Level Communications
- Ability to Generalize and Contextualize the NLP Master Practitioner Content and Skills to Other Fields of Personal Interest
- Degree of Integration of NLP Master Practitioner Content Knowledge and Skills

NLP Trainer

Training Structure

- The Trainer's Training is/was conducted by an INLPTA Master Trainer authorized to do so by the INLPTA Board of Directors
- The certification training meets INLPTA training structure requirements
- Minimum of 150 hours of formal course room training. (excluding breaks longer than 30 minutes)
- Minimum of 19 days of formal course room training
- The attended training meets the INLPTA accreditation competency standards and guidelines
- The certificate needs to be signed by at least two INLPTA NLP Master Trainers
- The certificates need to have the starting and ending dates, as well as the numbers of hours and dates written on them. And all certificates need to ordered by the international or national INLPTA coordinator and be numbered and sealed with the official INLPTA seal

General Criteria for NLP Trainer

- The candidate is of INLPTA NLP Master Practitioner accredited status
- The candidate has attended and successfully completed an INLPTA Trainers training
- The candidate has successfully met the INLPTA competency requirements for an INLPTA Trainer, assessed by at least two authorized INLPTA Trainer Trainers

- The candidate has successfully completed the following:
- Written assessment of intellectual integration of Practitioner, Master Practitioner, and Trainer content (at least 85% correct)
- Behavioral Assessment of presentation and training skill levels
- At least two (30 min.+) evaluated NLP presentations before an audience with feedback from the audience and the INLPTA Trainers Trainer
- An unannounced impromptu presentation and/or demonstration of an NLP content piece or technique before an audience
- Assessment of competency in training design
- Demonstrated attitude based on ecology, learning, and the living embodiment of the presuppositions of NLP
- It is strongly recommended that the candidate has either reviewed and/or assisted with a Practitioner and Master Practitioner program since their original training at those levels as a student
- It is strongly recommended that the candidate has received 20 hours of either personal coaching, supervision, or therapy by a certified INLPTA NLP Trainer

Intellectual and Behavioral Competencies

An INLPTA NLP Trainer is expected to demonstrate intellectual and behavioral competence in the following areas at appropriate levels of frames, principles, techniques, and distinctions:

- Excellence in attitudinal, behavioral, and intellectual competency in all Practitioner and Master Practitioner level skills and the demonstrated ability to do several patterns simultaneously at multiple levels

- Demonstrated ability to design a complete INLPTA Practitioner and Master Practitioner accreditation training
- Demonstrated ability to design and conduct the delivery of NLP content chunks
- Demonstrated ability to facilitate within students the learning of NLP content and the development of NLP skills and attitudes
- Demonstrated ability to establish and maintain excellent levels of rapport with all participants, colleagues and trainers
- Demonstrated ability to design and facilitate group inductions overtly and covertly
- Demonstrated ability to establish and maintain rapport with groups
- Demonstrated ability to work ecologically with groups
- Demonstrated ability to pace and lead a group in ecological directions
- Demonstrated ability to model the learner
- Demonstrated ability to pace, lead, incorporate and utilize the differences in world views between students-students and trainer-student(s)
- Demonstrated ability to utilize Satir Categories as applied to group communication
- Demonstrated ability to design, facilitate and debrief exercises
- Demonstrated ability to deliver instructions for exercises
- Demonstrated ability to demonstrate all Practitioner and Master Practitioner patterns overtly and covertly
- Demonstrated ability to establish and utilize stage anchors
- Demonstrated ability to design and deliver nested loops
- Demonstrated ability to answer questions and facilitate unconscious processes in an open frame
- Demonstrated ability to coach by facilitating unconscious learning processes

- Demonstrated ability to utilize environmental influences to facilitate optimum learning at conscious and unconscious levels
- Demonstrated ability to facilitate learning at different logical levels and of different logical types
- Demonstrated ability to design and conduct trainings that facilitate different adult learning styles
- Demonstrated ability to appropriately assess and evaluate students at Practitioner and Master Practitioner levels
- Behavioral demonstration of being able to "walk what you talk and talk what you walk"
- Excellent state control, emotional stability, stress resistance and self management
- Demonstrated ability to know and process your own model of the world and to adjust yourself congruently, ecologically, and respectfully to another person's model of the world
- Demonstrated ability to handle and resolve conflict, and to make effective and ecological decisions as appropriate to context
- Basic understanding of common knowledge models from psychology, physiology, brain research, therapy and other related areas to NLP
- Demonstrated ability to design, deliver and utilize metaphors in training
- Demonstrated ability to give and receive feedback in educative and self evolutionary ways
- Demonstrated ability to design, deliver and facilitate educative tasking
- Demonstrated ability to handle hecklers, under achievers, "problem" cases, ecological and/or ethical issues
- Demonstrated ability to calibrate groups and to respond accordingly
- Demonstrated ability to alter one's own training style as appropri-

ate to context, audience and outcome

NLP Master Trainer

NLP Master Trainers are recognized as having attained a superior level of training excellence in the domain of NLP Certification trainings. The request for entry to the assessment process must be accompanied with a personal voucher from the NLP Master Trainer with whom the applicant has trained.

General Criteria for NLP Master Trainer

- The candidate is an accredited INLPTA NLP Trainer
- The candidate has attended and successfully completed an INLPTA Master Trainer's Training as authorized by the INLPTA Board of Directors
- The candidate has successfully met the INLPTA competency requirements for an NLP Master Trainer, as assessed by the INLPTA Board of Directors

Training Excellence

Have fully conducted as the principal trainer a minimum of 5 NLP Certification Trainings consisting of at least one Practitioner and one Master Practitioner Certification Trainings. to INLPTA standards.

Dates of conducted trainings to be submitted to the INLPTA Board of Directors along with the signatures of the students who have attended

CHAPTER 10: NLP CERTIFICATIONS

those specific programs.

Have trained and accredited to INLPTA standards a minimum of 50 NLP Practitioners and 20 NLP Master Practitioners. This is to be monitored by the process of the NLP Trainer submitting to the INLPTA Board of Directors signed acceptance forms from each of their certified students for receipt of their Certificates, which are to be correlated to the number of INLPTA certificates and seals that have been requested by that NLP Trainer.

It is strongly recommended that the candidate has assisted and co-taught in an INLPTA Trainer's Training at least once (separate from the tasks encompassed within the Master Trainer's Track), and have received successful evaluations from a minimum of two INLPTA Board of Directors based on the degree of training expertise, content knowledge, and attitude.

Contribution to NLP

- The contribution constitutes a new technique or model of intervention for change that allows NLP to do something it could not do before, or could not do as easily, elegantly, or generatively.
- The contribution is able to be operationalized in a practical form
- The developer is to conduct a presentation of their contribution at an INLPTA International Conference if requested to do so
- INLPTA is given the rights to publish the contribution, with all due credit to the developer, for dissemination to the NLP community in the most appropriate form as determined by the INLPTA Board of Directors (with input from the INLPTA Board of Advisers)

AIP

The Association for Integrative Psychology, or AIP for short, was founded in 2005 by Matthew B. James, Ph.D. Its purpose is to promote awareness and acceptance of complementary, alternative, and integrative approaches as viable ways to facilitate change. A variety of disciplines is represented in the field of Integrative Psychology such as acupuncture, hypnosis, NLP, naturopathic medicine, and others.

Here are their standards for each of the NLP certifications:

NLP Practitioner

Duration of Training - Minimum of 120 hours of training in the basics of NLP. Taught by a Certified Master Practitioner of NLP under the supervision of a Certified Trainer of NLP, or a Certified Trainer of NLP, or a Certified Master Trainer of NLP.

Demonstration of the ability to identify the following basic skills, techniques, patterns and concepts of NLP and to utilize them successfully with self and others.

- Presuppositions of NLP
- Rapport
- Sensory Acuity

- Representational Systems
- Meta-Model
- Milton Model
- Elicitation of well-formed, ecological outcomes and structures of the present state.
- Metaphor Creation
- Frames
- Anchoring
- Dissociation and Association
- Logical Levels of Thinking
- Submodalities
- Reframing
- Strategies
- Parts Integration

NLP Master Practitioner

Duration of Training - Minimum of 120 hours of advanced NLP training. Taught by a Certified Trainer of NLP or a Certified Master Trainer of NLP. Minimum of 15 hours of direct trainer supervision.

Prerequisite: Must be at the Practitioner of NLP level.

Demonstration of the ability to identify the following basic skills, techniques, patterns, and concepts of NLP and to utilize these successfully with self and with others.

- All NLP Practitioner-level skills.
- Design individual interventions.

- Master Practitioner Skills
- Meta Programs
- Criteria (Values)
- sleight of mouth
- Installation and utilization of strategies
- Refined use of submodalities
- Negotiations
- Presentation skills
- Modeling

NLP Trainer

Duration of Training - Minimum of 120 hours of very advanced training. Taught by a Certified Master Trainer of NLP. Minimum of 15 hours of direct trainer supervision.

Must be at the Master Practitioner of NLP level.

Satisfactory behavioral demonstrations of the following:

- Successfully complete behavioral demonstrations in all Practitioner and Master Practitioner level skills, ability to do any and all practitioner and master practitioner techniques simultaneously both overtly and covertly.
- Demonstrate ability to shift between content and form (i.e. between experience and labeling).
- Ability to do (demonstrate the behavior of) what one is teaching, to teach what one is doing, to teach what one is doing and to label it linguistically (i.e. model self).

- Demonstration of Presentation and Teaching Skills:
- Pacing and leading
- Respect for the audience (i.e. at least keeping separate your's and other's model of the world, and responding to these congruently; considering and responding ecologically to others; conscious and unconscious processes).
- Answers questions that include discerning the level and intent of questions and generating level-appropriate responses.
- Design of presentation - At the least, setting opening and closing frames, setting outcomes, chunking, and sequencing of information and experience, balancing information - giving information and allowing occasions for discovery, and facilitating generalization of information and skills across context and time.
- Design of exercises - At the least, providing for both overt and covert learning in each exercise, including previously learned material for cumulative learning, specifying outcomes of exercises, providing a task for all involved persons ensuring behavioral learning, and including a future pace.
- Explanation of exercises including the ability to explain an exercise behaviorally without the use of notes or printed aids.
- Use of deep and shallow metaphors.
- Utilization of multi-level feedback - Ongoing re-evaluation and incorporation of overt and covert information from individuals and group.
- Graceful intervention in groups - At the least maintaining rapport and giving specific sensory grounded feedback, via questions that directionalize appropriate search to facilitate peoples discovery for themselves, demonstration, or if necessary, overtly telling them what to do.
- "Tasking" - the creation of a task that presupposes that a person behaves in a different way that expands his/her model of the world.

- Performs successful demonstrations.
- Demonstration of a personal style and artistry (indicating that the new trainer is integrating skills into his/her own behavior).
- Design in writing, a Practitioner and Master Practitioner NLP Training.

NLP Master Trainer

Duration of Training – Minimum of three (3) years as lead trainer in Practitioner and Master Practitioner NLP Trainings. Must be taught by a Certified Master Trainer of NLP.

Must be at the Trainer of NLP level.

Demonstration of the following behavioral competencies:

- Practitioner, Master Practitioner, and Trainer level of NLP knowledge and techniques.
- Lead Trainer in at least five (5) Practitioner of NLP Trainings. Proof of trainings necessary.
- Lead Trainer in at least three (3) Master Practitioner Trainings. Proof of trainings necessary.

Documentation of direct supervision by a Certified Master Trainer of NLP doing the training. The result of these evidential procedures would be that the Certified Master Trainer of NLP would "know" the candidate's knowledge, skills, and abilities as an NLP Trainer and would be able to attest to those areas. Documentation would include:

- Immediate and accurate recall and teaching of any NLP subject from memory (without written notes).
- Assisting and teaching at three (3) Master Practitioner of NLP Trainings that are taught by a Certified Master Trainer of NLP. Topics of instruction should show variety of material. Quality of instruction should be at satisfactory or higher. Proof and quality of instruction must be signed by the Certified Master Trainer of NLP.
- Assisting at three (3) consecutive Trainers Trainings for NLP. Proof of assistance with a listing of areas of responsibility that were performed and signed by the Certified Master Trainer of NLP.
- Able to think and discuss at least two (2) logical levels above the content of Trainer level of NLP.

During this process, demonstrate a willingness to learn how to improve his/her knowledge, skills, and abilities in NLP Training by having meetings/discussions with the Certified Master Trainer as needed.

There may be additional requirements that are more subjective and may be discussed with your Certified Master Trainer.

Must be approved by two (2) Master Trainers of NLP from different organizations.

Bibliography

Hall, L. M. (2016). *The Matrix Model: The Premier Systems Model of Neuro-Semantics.* (3rd ed.). NSP: Neuro-Semantic Publications.

Hall, L. M. (2012). *Meta-States* (3rd ed.). NSP: Neuro-Semantic Publications.

Dilts, R. (1998). *Modeling with NLP.* Dilts Strategy Group.

Hall, L. M., & Bodenhamer, B. G. (1997). *Figuring Out People: Design Engineering with Meta-Programs.* Crown House Publishing Ltd.

Robbie, E. (2000). The Ordering Principle of the Meta Model of NLP. *NLP World,* 7(3), 25-63.

Dilts, R., Grinder, J., Bandler, R., & Delozier, J. (1980). *Neuro-linguistic Programming: Volume 1.* Meta Publications.

Bodenhamer, B. G., & Hall, L. M. (2001). *The user's manual for the brain: The Complete Manual for Neuro-linguistic Programming Practitioner Certification.* Crown House Pub Limited.

Hall, L. M., & Battino, R. (1999). *The Sourcebook of Magic: A Comprehensive Guide to the Technology of NLP.* Crown House Publishing.

About the Author

Jacob Laguerre is the Founder of PCI Alpha, an online platform dedicated to the study and application of NLP, Personal Development, and related disciplines. He's a certified NLP Practitioner who's been studying and practicing NLP since 2015. He has taught over 2,000 students through his online courses. In his free time, he enjoys reading, learning new languages, working out, taking long walks, and contemplating the meaning of life.

You can connect with me on:
- https://pcialpha.com
- https://twitter.com/pcialpha
- https://facebook.com/pcialpha
- https://youtube.com/@pcialpha

Subscribe to my newsletter:
- https://pcialpha.com/mindmap

www.ingramcontent.com/pod-product-compliance
Lightning Source LLC
Chambersburg PA
CBHW072004150426
43194CB00008B/990